The Black Raven

The Black Raven:
A Study in the Folk Necromancy of Early Modern Germany
Copyright © 2025 Alexander Cummins & Brian Johnson
Cover artwork © Adeline Soothtell
All Rights Reserved.

ISBN 978-1-915933-70-6 (Hardcover)
ISBN 978-1-915933-71-3 (Softcover)

A CIP catalogue for this title is available from the British Library.
10 9 8 7 6 5 4 3 2 1

Published in 2025
Hadean Press
West Yorkshire
England
hadean.press

The Black Raven

A Study in the Folk Necromancy
of Early Modern Germany

by
ALEXANDER CUMMINS
and
BRIAN JOHNSON

Contents

I.

𝔉light of the 𝔅lack 𝔅aven

BIBLIOGRAPHIC PROLEGOMENON TO A FAUSTIAN SUBGENRE

The literary phenomenon surrounding a German magician calling himself Faustus, possibly born in the town of Helmstadt, Bavaria, where he was christened with the name Georg around 1466, began barely two decades after the probable death of this obscure historical figure in 1536.[1] While it was a series of pseudobiographical accounts published between 1587 and 1607 that brought the fully-formed Faustus legend into print,[2] the performance of Christopher Marlowe's *Doctor Faustus* as early as 1589 clearly indicates that the character and his mythos were already well established by that time.[3] Indeed, already in the 1550s, humorous accounts of Faustus's putative exploits—mainly involving magical tricks whereby he

---

[1] Davies (2009), 49–50. For what can be inferred about the historical Faustus, and the development of his legend during the sixteenth century, see Baron (2013) and van der Laan (2013).

[2] Henning and Paisey (1978), 1. The direct precursor to these publications was likely the so-called Wolfenbüttel manuscript, the main episodes of which are translated in Haile (1965).

[3] Honan (2005), 198–9.

gets the better of nobles and commoners alike, all very much in the vein of traditional folk entertainment—were being recorded in regional German chronicles.[4] By the late seventeenth century, the popular press had begun packaging tracts of wildly varied content—ghost stories and "wonders" of the natural world, almanacs, occult secrets and home remedies—together with literature like the *ärgerliche Leben und schreckliche Ende* of Johannes Faustus,[5] a practice which reflected, and probably contributed to, a certain degree of conflation between this kind of fantastical fiction and actual magical practices in the public imagination. This tendency would culminate in seventeenth-century Germany with conjuring books, in print as well as manuscript, bearing the name of Doctor Faustus.

We need look no further than the *Testament* of King Solomon, or the Iberian legacy of Saint Cyprian of Antioch, to find precedents for the weaving of an illustrious thaumaturgical forebear's more or less dramatized biography into a text of operative sorcery, a literary device employed since late antiquity by scribes seeking the justification of sanctity for their compilations of magical secrets. The genre of practical magical texts attributed to, named after, or otherwise associated with Faustus does not fully coalesce within the documentary record until the mid-1600s, by which point it indeed appears to have been heavily influenced by the popular magical handbooks of the preceding century and a half.[6]

---

4 van der Laan (2013), 130–1.

5 Doering-Manteuffel and Bachter (2004), 192–3.

6 Henning and Paisey (1978), 4–5.

Bearing little similarity to the more extraordinary feats of the *Faustbücher*'s fictionalized protagonist—flying to the stars, making Helen of Troy his concubine—the contents of these books more often recapitulate the relatively modest type of ritualized spirit coercion that had been typical of European grimoires since the late Middle Ages, with an overwhelming emphasis on recovering hidden treasure.

Just as the *Historia von D. Johann Fausten*, published by Johann Spies in 1587, was less a rigorously authentic portrayal of the historical *nigromancer*'s actual career, and more a product of the late sixteenth-century vogue for *Teufelsbücher* featuring sinners brought to (often humorous or ironic) ruination by the Devil,[7] so the proliferation of "Faustian" grimoires may have partly been a response to the *Bibliothèque bleue* pamphlets which had begun surreptitiously trickling across the French border into German Imperial territories, many of them bearing purported magical secrets.[8] The market demand for this newly available form of mass-produced occult knowledge in an era of increasing general literacy could well have motivated a domestic cottage industry in grimoire forgery. Ritual instructions and material preparations, titles and other framing material, could all be collected piecemeal, compiled, and re-transmitted back and forth between personal notebooks and cheap printed paperbacks.

Notwithstanding their superficial ascription of publication dates within Georg of Helmstadt's

---

7 Davies (2009), 50.

8 Davies (2009), 98, 121–2.

lifetime—or even earlier!—the tenuous relationship of the material found in books like *Der schwarze Rabe*, *Praxis Magica Faustiana*, and other *Höllen-Zwang* publications to the literary mythos of Faustus, to say nothing of the historical man, forces the philologist to concede that any attempt to construct a distinct classification of these texts on the basis of a shared magical methodology may be begging the question. When we see the fictional Faustus go to a crossroads in the forest outside Wittenberg to draw a circle where he summons a spirit who confronts him with all manner of terrifying phenomena—winds, phantasmagoric apparitions, pyrotechnics—until Faustus "conjured him by his master...compelling him to fulfill his desire",[9] we certainly aren't witnessing anything novel in terms of what one might find in many a sixteenth-century grimoire. If we recognize that the whole literary edifice of the Faustus legend was an organic outgrowth of a culture already thoroughly familiar with the idea of the black-art book, then arbitrarily circumscribing early-modern German vernacular grimoires under the name of that particular peripatetic conjuror begins to look like something of a category mistake.

Little as the practical contents of these books may have truly distinguished them from hundreds of similar compilations that had been produced and re-produced across Western Europe for several centuries, there are the occasional stylistic flourishes which do set the German corpus apart. One motif that surfaces with recognizable frequency is the "black raven",

---

9 Haile (1965), 24–6.

often in the form of an inset illustration of the black bird, sometimes lending *schwarze Rabe* to a work's title, and occasionally prefacing its diabolical secrets with a few lines of rhymed couplets to warn/entice would-be readers.[10] One of this corvid's earliest verifiable appearances came near the last quarter of the eighteenth century, illustrated sitting atop a book in a cheaply-printed edition of *D. Fausts Original Geister Commando* (another oft-copied title, here claiming a publication date of 1510).[11] Again, in 1815, the secretary of the Dresden Royal Library was approached repeatedly with requests for *Die goldne Tabella Rabellina* (a title also cited within the aforementioned *Geister Commando*), said to feature a similar image, albeit this one carrying a ring in its beak[12]—a depiction which neatly closes our bibliographic circle, echoing as it does the frontispiece of the unique manuscript version of *Der schwarze Rabe* which forms the basis of the present study.

While the popularity of the raven-and-ring motif perhaps owes more to the inherent exigencies of the highly mimetic grimoire medium than it does to any deeper occult significance, the origin of the image may lie with a codicological mystery of a different sort. Ever since the Ottoman capture of Buda, capital

---

10 See Universitäts- und Landesbibliothek Darmstadt, Hs. 2543, 2r; Scheible (1846), 853–4.

11 Davies (2009), 121; Henning and Paisey (1978) is a more detailed bibliographic analysis of this publication.

12 Ebert (1830), 576. One further example of the raven illustration accompanies the text of *Dr. Johann Faustens Mircul-Kunst- und Wunder-Buch* (allegedly dated to 1469) printed in Scheible (1846), 852.

of the Kingdom of Hungary, in 1526, and well into the nineteenth century,[13] the imaginations of scholars and bibliophiles across Europe had been gripped by accounts of the marvelous library said to have been assembled there by the late king, Matthias Hunyadi, called "Corvinus" for the ring-bearing raven depicted on his family's armorial crest—and on the frontispieces of his books.[14] While the king, typical of his age, was fascinated with astrology (his library's ceiling as well as some of its books bore horoscopic illuminations marking significant inaugural moments),[15] and furnished his collection with works by Ptolemy as well as his own court astronomer, Johann Tolhopf[16]—not to mention receiving the translations (and effusive praise) of Marsilio Ficino along with a copy of the Florentine's *De vita libri tres*[17]—among the library's holdings, extant or reputed, there appears nothing quite so esoteric as actual necromancy, or even any of the more outré titles pseudonymously attributed to Aristotle.[18] Nevertheless, legends grow in the telling, and tend to accrue to themselves sufficiently fabulous appendages to fill any capacity that the bare facts of history leave wanting. If any occult philosopher chanced to read Johannes Brassicanus's enraptured description of the Corvinian

---

13 Tanner (2008), xvi.

14 Tanner (2008), 25.

15 Csapodi (1969), 16.

16 Tanner (2008), 6, 99–100.

17 Tanner (2008), 4, 114.

18 See Tanner, 216–224 for a list of extant manuscripts attributed to the Corvinian library.

library upon his return to Vienna shortly before Buda fell to Suleiman the Magnificent,[19] they might have been forgiven for supposing that the place had contained the very teachings of Hermes Trismegistus written in his own hand. Little wonder, then, if grimoire copyists in the German-speaking lands began appropriating the hallmark of such a trove of rarefied (now lost) knowledge to their own manuscripts.

Our own *Black Raven*, Universitäts- und Landesbibliothek Darmstadt, Hs. 2543, is an anonymous German handschrift, drafted on paper in black ink, its title page bearing a simple, if well-executed, drawing of the eponymous bird holding a ring in its beak. Though it appears to have once belonged in the collection of a Darmstadt councilor named Karl Wunderlich (1769–1841),[20] the booklet's precise place and date of origin are as obscure as its author—as we've seen, the self-professed publication information of such texts is not to be taken at face value. Palaeography is little help in this regard (at least to the non-specialist), since the *Kurrentschrift* script in which the manuscript's thirty-four numbered pages are largely written remained remarkably consistent from the fifteenth century well into the twentieth. The Darmstadt manuscript itself seems somewhat confused on this point, with the date of composition shifting from 30 July, 1519 on the title page to 15 April, 1515 in the explicit, though both inscriptions agree that it came from Passau. Claims to imaginary antiquity aside,

---

19 Tanner (2008), 171.
20 Doering-Manteuffel and Bachter (2004), 196–7.

however, the writer's orthography may offer some clues. Comparing several archaic spelling conventions employed throughout the text against usage patterns in the German printed corpus for the years 1500 to the present (and assuming these spellings are, in fact, archaic, and not just idiosyncratic), the manuscript can very likely be dated to some time prior to the mid-nineteenth century. If we also assume that the author's literary evocation of the "black raven" is playing upon the established grimoire tradition transmitted under that name, then we can tentatively narrow down the manuscript's provenance to 1775–1840, which, as grimoires go, is actually remarkably precise.

This dating would also further place some of the scribal habits and other visual elements evinced by the *Raven* into dialogue with the typographic and pictorial norms of the printed grimoires circulating in eighteenth-century Germany. The *Nigromantisches Kunst-Buch*,[21] for instance—plausibly published, as the title page claims, at Köln in 1743—uses a Roman typeface to differentiate its Latin words and phrases from the surrounding German *Fraktur* (a distinction introduced almost contemporaneously with the invention of the Fraktur typeface itself in the sixteenth century), just as the *Raven* renders proper names and Latin vocabulary

---

21 *Nigromantisches Kunst-Buch, handelnd von der Glücks-Ruthe, dem Ring und der Krone Salomonis, den Fürsten-Geheimnissen, den dienstbaren Krystall- und Schatz-Geistern und andern wunderbaren Arcanen : Nach einer Handschrift aus der Bibliothek eines Fürst-Abtes im vorigen Jahrhundert wortgetreu und mit allen Abbildungen veröffentlicht : Der wahrhaftige englische Schlüssel Salomonis ... / Nach dem wahren Original verdeutscht und mit Abbildungen.*

in an italic script that is instantly distinguishable from the Kurrentschrift of the German text. Another German magical manuscript of the eighteenth century, the para-necromantic *Tractatus de Arte Phythonica*,[22] follows much the same chirographic pattern in citing the patriarchs, spirits, and names of God stipulated for its ritual skull-interrogation. Magicians have been incorporating material from printed sources into their personal, handwritten *vades mecum* ever since the relevant texts began to become more widely available in that form than they had ever been in manuscript (a process Owen Davies has characterized as the "democratisation of learned magic"[23]), and it is not surprising that they—like most literate individuals in text-saturated post-Gutenberg cultures—would adopt some of the structural elements of print when organizing their own *mise en pages* as well.

The pamphlet's contents are rather more reticent than its formal elements in offering leads: the conjuring procedures described are not deeply liturgical (at no point is one required to attend Mass, for example), but they don't betray any particular post-Reformation bias either, freely invoking intercessory saints and evincing a blithe disregard for Protestant doctrinal strictures on the soul's disposition after death. The more explicitly sorcerous materials similarly float rather freely in the chronological continuum. The piecemeal construction of a paper or parchment circle, attested at least as early as the fourteenth-century *Liber Iuratis Honorii*,

22 Universitätsbibliothek Leipzig, Cod. mag. 97.
23 Davies (2023).

had become a popular mode of operation amongst the exorcism manuals of portability-conscious eighteenth- and nineteenth-century German treasure hunters[24]—to say nothing of at least one rag-tag party of Englishmen a few centuries prior.[25] Likewise, the names of planetary angels which the *Raven* shares with the 1303 *Conciliator differentiarum philosophorum et medicorum* of Peter d'Abano are the same as those appearing in pseudo-Peter's *Heptameron* in the 1500s,[26] and the seven *Obersten* of the Darmstadt manuscript, identical with the Olympian governors of the sixteenth-century *Arbatel*, are again a common feature of the aforementioned popular handbooks.[27]

Regarding its place of origin, the evidence of the manuscript is both obscure and allusive. Further irregular spellings may point to the influence of dialects belonging to varieties of German both High and Low, posing intriguing questions as to the author's own homeland, travels, and breadth of (in)formal education. The pseudepigraphic Passau inscription is telling, but not because it places the book geographically; rather, it situates the *Raven* within the discursive universe of the early-modern German occultists who read and copied grimoires of its ilk. Again and again, the name of this Bavarian city on the Danube graces the cover pages of tracts and compilations with titles invoking the

---

24 Cf. Horst (1821), 81; Scheible (1849), 200–1.

25 Klaassen and Hubbs Wright (2021), passim; see also Rankine (2009), 125.

26 Thorndike (1923), 900; Peterson (2021), 207 ff.

27 Cf. Peterson (2009), 29; Horst (1821), 119.

imprimatur of Faustus or an enigmatic avian.[28] One such manuscript, the richly illustrated *Praxis Magica Faustiana*, which has been conjectured to lie especially early in the tradition of Faustian magic books—and uncharacteristically near its nominal date of 1527[29]— may have started the trend. Cities like Wittenberg and Toledo had long borne reputations (earned or not) as centers of occult learning and, hence, publishing, and fanciful ascriptions to that effect were something of a conspiratorial wink between those in-the-know bibliophiles who circulated this kind of dangerous literature. By the turn of the nineteenth century, Passau too had taken its place in the pantheon of their coded mythology.

---

28 *Der schwarze Rabe* (Passau, 1519/1515); *D. Iohannis Faustii Magia Naturalis Et Innaturalis; oder unerforschlicher Höllen-Zwang...* (Passau, 1612); *Doctoris Johannis Fausti Cabalae Nigrae* (Passau, 1505); *Praxis Magica Faustiana: oder der von Doct Iohann Faust. Practicirte und beschworne Höllen Zwang* (Passau, 1527).

29 Herzogin Anna Amalia Bibliothek, Hs. Q 455; see van der Laan (2013), 126–7.

II.

[scan #4: 2r]

𝕿𝖍𝖊 𝕭𝖑𝖆𝖈𝖐 𝕽𝖆𝖛𝖊𝖓.
Passau,
30 July, 1519.

The black raven who is not bound
here the golden ring has found,
and so I rest me without shame
for the black raven is my name.[30]

[#6: 3r]

On the
Blessing and Conjuration
of the Circle.

When the circle with all pertinent things is prepared
as usual, from parchment or virgin paper,[31] which one
must bless and conjure, then place two consecrated
wax candles thereupon and suffumigate, then say:
In the name of ✠✠✠ *Amen!*
*I, NN, bless and conjure this circle by the name of the great,
mighty, and*

---

30 The German text opens with two quasi-nonametric
rhymed couplets. I have attempted to retain the style of verse,
if not the specific meter and rhyme-sounds of the original.

31 Compare *Liber Juratus* cxxvii: 'Thus with your circle
complete, exit and write outside in the earth or on small
pieces of parchment, the seven names of the creator...'; also
the method of the so-called Mixindale fellowship discussed
in Klaassen and Hubbs Wright, *The Magic of Rogues.*

[#7: 3v]

omnipotent threefold God and his most holy majesty, and by the words of power Agla, Adonai, Tetragrammaton, Sadai, Zebaoth, Paracletos, Jehova, Emanuel, Alpha et[32] *Omega; I conjure you evil spirits as well by the words of power now spoken in the name of Jesus, that you shall absolutely not damage nor violate this circle, nor cause the least harm by accident or affliction to either me or my companions, neither in body nor soul, so*

[#8: 4r]

I command all of you spirits in the name of the most holy Trinity. Amen.

[33]Ja.za.ri. A✠Ha✠na_et
✠Seraph✠Soehliel xe_se
_pha✠Phaiamech✠Salma-
sace✠ve.sar✠Actu.ar✠
Pe.li.ar.so.nor✠Lan.clei.
✠Ja.za.ri.el✠La.tis.ten
a.za.re.et✠Scheliel✠Zu-
ri✠A.za.mel✠Egivi✠et
Verchiel✠Amuziel✠Selo-
el✠Eno.di.el✠Hamali-
el✠Requeel✠Zeaphliel.

---

32 Note that I've left untranslated the Latin words and phrases in the various invocations, since presumably the writer distinguished them thus from the surrounding German text with the intention that they be recited as-is.

33 The following text may in fact represent the inscription for the circle.

✠O.sach.y✠Na.ma.chay.
✠Na.riel✠Haniel✠Ra_

[#9: 4v]
phael✠O.ri.phi.el.

Concerning these words, always divide by the ✠ and
demarcate each syllable distinctly, and thereby one
can read everything back again.

And hereby I conjure this circle in the name of Jesus, Amen.

[#10: 5r]
Then, now that this circle is consecrated and you wish
to begin summoning, you shall go therein with your
companions and say: *The Lord protect our proceeding
and our lives* — previously having examined your

companions as to whether they by chance are sunk
in grave sin, so that perhaps they can be answered by
your apt reproaches, and you and your companions
do not thereby come to misfortune – then you shall
begin the

[#11: 5v]
work with the following prayer, and proceed with the
summoning of the spirit which you wish to have.

The First Prayer.
O, almighty, eternal, merciful God, beloved heavenly father,
who knows the hearts of men, and knows their need and
their entreaty better than they themselves can say it to you. O,
you king of all kings and lord of all lords and director of the
whole world, we your children beg

[#12: 6r]
humbly, with meek spirit, that you shall wish to give us
luck, health, and blessing, in this our plan and work, and to
send your holy angels to help us, Michael, Gabriel, Samael,
Raphael, Sachiel, Anael, and Casiel, who before your holy
throne ceaselessly cry, 'Holy, holy, holy is our Lord, God
of Hosts, Heaven and Earth are full of His glory'; help us
beloved Lord and God and be gracious to us

[#13: 6v]
in all our need, hear our appeal and protect us from all evil,
Amen.

Hereupon pray a devout Our Father.

The Second Prayer.
O, you great, holy, and almighty God, beloved heavenly father in Heaven. I beg you by

[#14: 7r]
Jesus Christ your only-begotten beloved son, and your holy names Agla, Adonai, Tetragrammaton, Eloah, Sother, Emanuel, that you shall wish in this covenant to give strength and power to the words of my mouth over the evil angels who have been cast out of your holy Heaven into the Abyss, that I may compel and bind them to appear visibly in friendly human form before my circle,

[#15: 7v]
and to fully satisfy my words and prayer, by the holy names of your godly majesty, Ja ✠ Adonai ✠ Ara ✠ Auray ✠ Ella ✠ Amalen ✠ Eisoi ✠ Vision ✠ Ehel ✠ Heer ✠ Agla ✠ that are conferred upon me, O you merciful God and beloved heavenly father, by Jesus Christ in the strength of the Holy Spirit, Amen.

Now follows the summons.
Note that in this summons naught but a few devils

[#16: 8r]

shall be called. They are of many different sorts, like
Lucifer and Beelzebub, these being the infernal gods.
The 7 kings who stem from their infernal gods are the
principals, and have under themselves certain crowns
and lordships, and they are Astaroth, Egim, Paimon,
Mastroth, Asrica, Storey, Cavocnz. These 7 kings
have subdued 7 princes, whose regency alternates.
These 7 princes are called Bareham,

[#17: 8v]

Harthan, Gannax, Ambuma, Juhbarmon, Harabejes,
Mayton, these having under them another 7 officers,
who are: Nepista, Phize, Aziabel, Harduel, Huiguil,
Hachiel, Daruel.

Summons and Conjuration.
Over the foremost devils Lucifer ✠ Beelzebub ✠ Paymon ✠
Kirie ✠ Emanuel ✠ ͡Fᴇ Eman ✠ Sachriel ✠ Galalandema
✠ Jehova ✠ Sume ✠ Deus ✠ omnes ✠ spiritus ✠

[#18: 9r]

My God, my God, protect me ⍾

Beelzebub et Lucifer, dugam,[34] *dugam.*

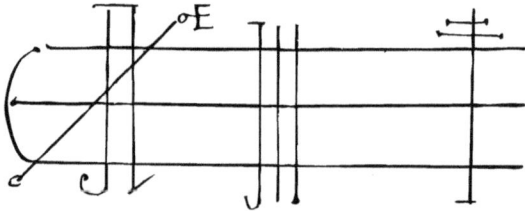

Ta.vac✠*Lucifer*✠*Rual*✠*Paymon et omnes spiritus*

[#19: 9v]
verite per signum Crucis, Kirie✠*Cassiel*✠*Salmazan*
Tetromion Ben Sancta Trinitas Eschretus[35] *Christus*✠ *Tarae*
Kirie Eleison✠
I conjure you Lucifer and Beelzebub, you two officers of the
devils, conjure you mightily once more by the great, almighty,
living, holy, and undivided God, the creator of Heaven and

---

34 Possibly a mangled rendering of Latin 'ducam'.

35 This series of words may derive from a mis-copying of
the phrase 'per sancta trinitas excretus' at some point in the
text's transmission history.

the Earth, yea I conjure you by all the holiness of God, by all the holy names

[#20: 10r]
of God, by all of holy creation, that you immediately compel and bind for me the spirit N before my circle, and command him to attend to my words, and to perform those same instructions, and to appear to me in a pleasant human form, and to fulfill my will and command in all things, and you shall guarantee this, Lucifer and Beelzebub, along with all your followers, commanded by the words of power Tetragrammaton Sother

[#21: 10v]
Deus Azetan Hott, Menean Trensie Zamay, el Lazamen, Deus Juebatha, Sacraman, Fiat Fiat Fiat! So be it! Gracious and merciful God protect me. You shall have no rest before these two, but rather nothing but fear, malediction, and terror shall assail you until you disobedient spirits obey me and are ready to fulfill my will. Fiat, Fiat, Fiat.

✠✠✠

[#22: 11r]
This is the sign of Lucifer and Beelzebub, for each spirit has their own sign.

Lucifer

SE} ⊐ᶜ ⅋

Beelzebub.

Now follows the summoning of Aciel the master of treasures.

[#23: 11v]
In the name of God the Father, the Son, and the Holy Spirit, Amen!

I, N, summon and conjure you, spirit Aciel, by Jesus Christ the judge of the living and the dead, by the creator of Heaven and the Earth, and by the great names of God

and high words of power Jehova Elohim Adonay Agla El
Tetragrammaton,

[#24: 12r]
that you, spirit Aciel, ⌐ †Ɛ ⅁ *in this instant appear before*
my circle, and speak with me in a friendly form in my
familiar language, without any fright, harm, or storm; come,
come, come! I conjure you, spirit Aciel, you who are a lord
over all hidden treasures of the earth, by the powerful words
and names Set, Schemhamphoras Dugam Dugam Dugam,
that

[#25: 12v]
you, spirit Aciel, fetch out this hidden treasure, which has
been displaced from human hands, from the same place where
it lies, and lay it beside this circle without any terror, fright,
hail, deceit, or blinding, nor harm to the circle nor my and
my companions' bodies and souls, this I command you. Come!
Come! Come!
Sacro✠Sancta✠Trinitas✠

I command you Aciel in

[#26: 13r]
the name of

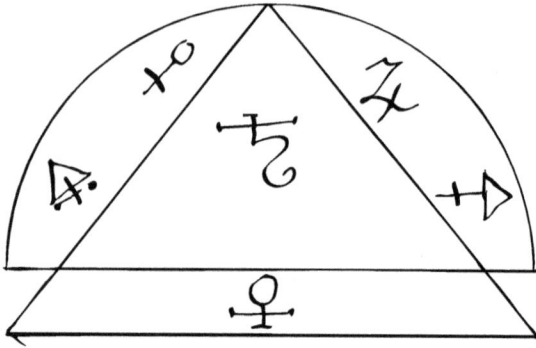

Nisza✠Hagal✠Ligkama
Raphael✠
Come! Come! Come!
Fiat! Fiat! Fiat!
Ducam, Ducam, Ducam,
Veni! Veni! Veni!

Spiritus Aciel
Signum
Spiritus Aciel

[#27: 13v (p. 24)]

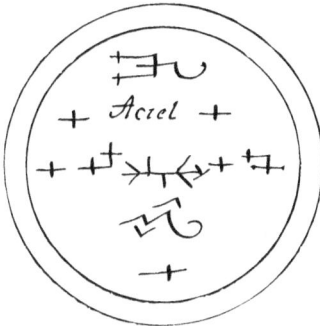

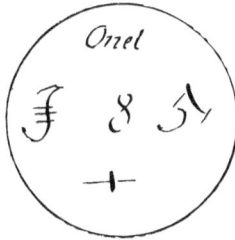

Crucis Christi vincit

[#28: 14r]

He

In the name of God the Father, the Son, and the Holy Spirit.
I conjure you by the most holy Trinity, you acclaimed angel,
you who are cast out from the throne of God, you who shall
be weighted down along with a thousand souls, you who have
been cast into the torment of Hell, and have been forsworn
from the womb, and I too have come to that place by the
Devil's power, and

[#29: 14v]
appoint to this place from beneath their heavy burden
Adonai, the high prince Gabriel, the prince Ninive, the prince
Adonai,[36] and their emissaries, and you, holy Niniverus, have
been joined with them, and so the Devil shall not divide you,
and so the Devil shall not divide you ✠✠✠.

Summoning of a Haunting Spirit.[37]
Haunting spirit, who dwells in this house (or barn), I, N,
conjure you in the name of the 14 Holy

---

36 *Sic.*

37 *Stammgeist*; a vanishingly rare word in the printed
corpus prior to c. 1810, its semantic ambiguity allowed for
a stark bifurcation in usage: frequently employed in an
ethno-national or political sense to characterize the 'spirit'
of a people (an early example appears in Arnold H. L.
Heeren's *Ideen über die Politik, den Verkehr und den Handel der
vornehmsten Völker der alten Welt*, 1793), it was also applied to
lingering spirits—ghosts who found themselves 'rooted' to a
particular place—such as may preside over hidden treasure
(several accounts of dealings with which Wilhelm F. Bischoff
adduces in *Die Geisterbeschwörer im neunzehnten Jahrhundert
oder die Folgen des Glaubens an Magie aus Untersuchungs-Acten
dargestellt vom Großherzoglich Sächs*, 1823). While sometimes
translated as 'tribal spirit' in the necromantic literature (cf.
Álvarez Ortiz, 2016), I believe the element *Stamm-* in this
context more closely pertains to the spirit's frequenting
of, or 'rootedness' in, a particular place, as in compounds
like *Stammgast* and *Stammkneipe*, hence I render the word in
English as 'haunting spirit'.

[#30: 15r]
Helpers,[38] *by the strength and power of God in Heaven and on Earth, and by the strength and power of all the holy angels in Heaven, and by the prayer of the whole Church;*[39] *and the sacrosanct Trinity shall threaten and compel you until you appear to me visibly in your true human form, and have neither peace nor rest until you fulfill my will.*

3 Our Fathers.[40]

Greeting of the Spirit.

[#31: 15v]
Be welcome you defiant spirit, for though you are willful, I wish to accommodate you.

If he then gives speech and answer, ask him if he would be released from his circumstances, and by what means he may be set free, and at what time and hour he would be put at liberty. Then, when this is finished, send him on his way again and say:
Go there in the peace of the Lord, the peace of God

---

38 A group of intercessory saints, the collective veneration of whom originated in the Rhineland during an outbreak of plague in the fourteenth century.

39 *Geistenheit.*

40 That is, recite the Lord's Prayer, or *Pater Noster*, three times.

[#32: 16r]

which is higher than all human reason and all ghostly capability, may it be between me and you as a firewall and a separation, such that we do not come together, and you can do me no harm, of which I and you would repent. In nomine Dei patris et filii et spiritus sancti, amen!

This dismissal must be said 3 times.

The most holy Trinity stand by me.

[#33: 16v]

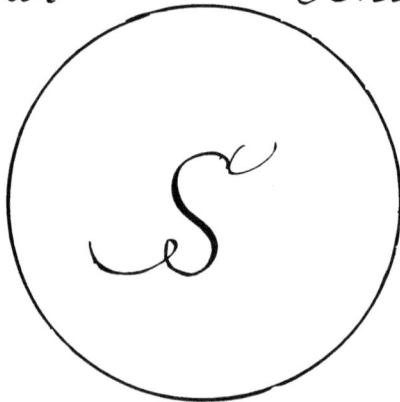

Now follow the names of the holy angels,[41] along with their planetary sigils:

1 ☉ Michael
2 ☽ Gabriel
3 ♂ Samiel
4 ☿ Raphael

[#34: 17r (p. 31)]
5 ♃ Sachiel
6 ♀ Anael
7 ♄ Casiel
These are the 7 Kings.

Names of the 7 Officers.[42]

Aratron — Derdiel
Bethor — Miseriel
Phalig — Seraphiel
Och — Asfariel
8 ♎ Hagith — Salomiel
7 ♒ Ophiel — Sateriel
11 ♏ Pfuel — Jachiel

---

41 This sequence of names is ultimately derived from Peter d'Abano's *Conciliator differentiarum philosophorum et medicorum*, diff. 9; see Thorndike, *A History of Magic and Experimental Science*, volume II, p. 900. A similar list, albeit reversing the attributions of Sol and Mercury, circulated independently, and was probably Agrippa's source for *De Occulta Philosophia*, e.g. 'The Scale of the Number Seven'.

42 Cf. *Arbatel*, aphorism 16.

There follow 12 spirits, with the sigils[43] in which

they are to be called on each day of the week.[44]

		Sunday	Monday	Tuesday	Wednesday	Thursday	Friday	Saturday
1	Maduth	☉	☽	♂	☿	♃	♀	♄
2	Janor	♀	♄	☉	☽	♂	☿	♃
3	Sullu	☿	♃	♀	♄	☉	☽	♂
4	Nusma	☽	♂	☿	♃	♀	♄	☉
5	Sedethi	♄	☉	☽	♂	☿	♃	♀
6	Thumen	♃	♀	♄	☉	☽	♂	☿
7	Curen	♂	☿	♃	♀	♄	☉	☽
8	Taris	☉	☽	♂	☿	♃	♀	♄
9	Neroa	♀	♄	☉	☽	♂	☿	♃
10	Jaxon	☽	♂	☿	♄	♀	♃	☉
11	Abur	☿	♃	♀	♄	☉	☽	♂
12	Nulbuon	☉	☽	♂	☿	♃	♄	♀

---

43 I.e., of the corresponding planetary hours.

44 The attribution of a unique spirit to each hour of each day of the week is a venerable practice (see the many recensions of the *Magical Treatise of Solomon*), but the method here is greatly simplified—a particular spirit is assigned to the same chronological hour of each weekday.

[#36: 18r]
Herein you will have found the spirits to fulfill all
that you will, and those who hand over treasure, but
if the spirits wish to cause much trouble, or to make
demands, then you must by no means allow them,
and on your life do not comply, lest you come to great
misfortune.

So, you have in this book an extraordinary treasure,
my good exorcist, which you must hold in esteem and
high honor, for

[#37: 18v]
by means of the same you can now bind and compel
and conjure the spirits, such that they shall serve you
perfectly, and must bring to you everything. Farewell.

Passau, 15 April, 1515.[45]

---

45 Cf. the date on the title page.

III.

[scan #4: 2r]

Der Schwarze Rabe.
Passau,
Anno 1519. d. 30 July.[46]

Der schwarze Rab so nicht gebunden
hat hier den goldene Ring gefunden
das rühe ich mich auch ohne Schand'
daß ich der schwarze Rab genannt.

[#6: 3r]

Von der
Einsegnung und Beschwörung
des Kreises.
Wenn der Kreis mit allen
zugehörigen Dingen wie ge-
wöhnlich verfertigt ist, von Per-
gamant oder Jungfern Pa-
pier, so muß man denselben
einsegnen und beschwören,
alsdenn zwei geweihte Wachs-
kerzen darauf sezen[47] und be-
rauchern, alsdann sprechen:

---

46 Variant of the standard German *Juli*, briefly competing
with the more common spelling c. 1790–1820. The author
frequently (if inconsistently) follows now-archaic or
formerly regional orthographic conventions. The following
chronological estimates for orthographic usage are based on
the Google ngram German (2019) corpus, 1500–2019.

47 Var. *setzen*, c. 1750–1870.

Im Nahmen[48] ✠✠✠ Amen!
Ich NN segne und beschwöre
diesen Kreis bei dem Nahmen
des grosen, gewaltigen und al-

[#7: 3v]

mächtigen dreininigen Gottes und seiner allerheiligsten
Majestät, und durch die Machtworte Agla, Adonai, Tetragrammaton, Sadai, Zebaoth, Paracletos, Jehova, Emanuel, Alpha et Omega, beschwöre ich
euch böse Geister, auch durch
jezt[49] gesprochene Machtworte
im Namen Jesu, daß ihr
diesen Kreis durchaus nicht
beschadiget noch verlezet,[50]
auch weder mir noch meinen
Gesellen, weder am Leib oder
Seele einigen Schaden Unfall
oder Leid zufüget, das gebiete

[#8: 4r]

ich euch Geister alle in den Na-
man der allerheiligsten .3.
faltigkeit. Amen.
Ja.za.ri. A✠Ha✠na_et

---

48 Var. *Namen*, c. 1580–1850.

49 Var. *jetzt*, c. 1750–1880.

50 Var. *verletzet*, c. 1630–1810.

✠Seraph✠Soehliel xe_se
_pha✠Phaiamech✠Salma-
sace✠ve.sar✠Actu.ar✠
Pe.li.ar.so.nor✠Lan.clei.
✠Ja.za.ri.el✠La.tis.ten
a.za.re.et✠Scheliel✠Zu-
ri✠A.za.mel✠Egivi✠et
Verchiel✠Amuziel✠Selo-
el✠Eno.di.el✠Hamali-
el✠Requeel✠Zeaphliel.
✠O.sach.y✠Na.ma.chay.
✠Na.riel✠Haniel✠Ra_

[#9: 4v]

phael✠O.ri.phi.el.
<In> diese Worte unterschei-
de allezeit bei dem ✠
und geschiefert jede Sÿlbe[51]
apart, damit man auch
alles wieder zurück lesen
kann.

---

51 Archaic var. *Silbe*, predominant (as *Sylbe*) until c. 1860;
ÿ-spelling possibly influenced by Dutch/Low German.

Und hiermit beschwöre ich diesen Kreis im Namen Jesu An

[#10: 5r]

Nachdem du nun dieser
Kreis also eingeweihet und
anfangen willst zu citiren,[52]
so gehe hinein samt deiner
Gesellen und spriche: Der
Herr behüte unsere Ein-
gang und Leibgang, zuvor
prüfe uber deine Gesellen
wohl, ob solche etwa im gra-
ben Sünden steken, damit
solche bei allenfalsigen Vor-
würfen von dir beantwor-
tet werden können und
du und deine Gesellen
dadurch nicht im Unglück
komst, alsdann fange das

[#11: 5v]

Werk mit folgendem Gebet
an, und fahre fort mit der
Citation des Geistes welchen
du haben willst.
Das erste Gebet.
O, allmächtiger, ewiger,
barmherziger Gott, lieber
himmlischer Vater, der du

---

52 From Latin *citatio.*

die Herzen der Menschen ken-
nest und ihre Noth[53] und
ihr Anliegen bester weißt
als sie dir es sagen können
O, du König aller Könige
und Herr aller Herrn und
Zegierer[54] der ganzen Welt,
wir deine Kinder bitten

[#12: 6r]

dich demüthiglich mit sauft-
muthigem Geist, du wollest
uns Glück Heil und Segen
geben, zu diesen unsern
Vorhaben und Werk und uns
zu Hülfe senden, deine heilige Engel, Michael, Gabriel
Samael, Raphael, Sachiel,
Anael und Casiel, die vor
deinem heiligen Thron ohne
Unterlaß rufen, heilig, heilig heilig ist unser Herr
Gott Sabaoth, Himmel und
Erde sind seiner Ehren voll,
hilf uns lieber Herr und
Gott und seÿ[55] uns gnädig

---

53 Archaic var. *Not*, predominant until c. 1890.
54 *Sic*; cf. *Zeigerer*.
55 Archaic var. *sei*, predominant (as *sey*) until c. 1835.

[#13: 6v]

im aller Noth, erhöre unsern Bitte und behüte uns
von allem Übel, Amen.
Hierauf bete ein andächtig
Vater Unser.

Das zweite Gebet
O, du groser heiliger und
Allmächtiger Gott, lieber
himmelischer Vater im Himmel. Ich bitte dich durch

[#14: 7r]

Jesum Christum deinen ein-
gebohrnen allerliebsten Sohn,
und deine heilige Nahmen
Agla, Adonai, Tetragrammaton, Eloah, Sother Emanu-
el, du wollest in dieser
Bunde den Worten meines
Mundes Kraft und Macht
geben, über die bösen En-

gel welche du von deinem
heiligen Himmel in den
Abgrund verstoßen hast,
daß ich sie möge zwingen
und binden sichtbarlich in
freundlicher Menschen Ge-
stalt vor meinem Kreis

[#15: 7v]

zu erscheinen, und meinen
Worten und Gebet völlig
nachzukommen, bei den heiligen Namen deiner göttli-
chen Majestät Ja✠Adonai✠
Ara✠Auray✠Ella✠Ama-
len✠Eisoi✠Vision✠Ehel✠
Heer✠Agla✠ das verleihe
mir o du barmherziger Gott
und lieber himmlischer Vater, durch Jesum Christum
in Kraft des Heiligen Geistes
Amen.
Nun folget die Citation.
Merk daß in dieser Citation
nichts als ein paar Teufel

[#16: 8r]

citiert werden. Es sind deren vielerlay Sorten, als
Lucifer und Beelzebub, dieses sind die höllischen Götter.
Die 7. Könige welche von ih-

ren Gottern der Hölle aus-
gehen sind die vornehmsten
und haben unter sich ge-
wisse Kronen und Herrschaf-
ten, als Astaroth Egim
Paimon, Mastroth, As-
rica, Storey, Cavocnz. Diesen 7. Königen sind 7. Fürsten unterworfen, deren
Regente abwechselnd. Diese
7. Fürsten heißen Bare-

[#17: 8v]

ham, Harthan, Gannax,
Ambuma, Juhbarmon, Ha-
rabejes, Mayton, diese haben unter sich noch 7. Obersten, welche sind Nepista,
Phize, Aziabel, Harduel,
Huiguil, Hachiel, Daruel.
Citation und Be-
schwörung.
Über die obersten Teufel
Lucifer✠Beelzebub✠Pay-
mon✠Kirie✠Emanuel✠
$\mathcal{CE}$ Eman✠Sachriel✠Ga-
lalandema✠Jehova✠Su-
me✠Deus✠omnes✠Spi-
ritus✠

[#18: 9r]

Mein Gott, Mein Gott feÿ[56]

mir

Be-
elzebub et Lucifer, dugam
dugam.

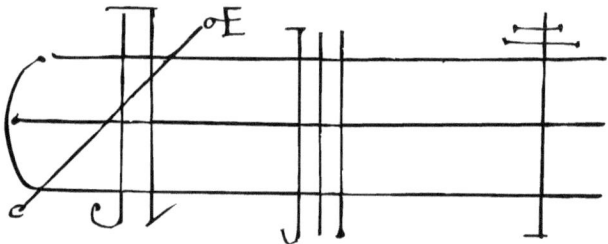

Ta.vac✠Lucifer✠Rual✠
Paymon et omnes spiritus

---

56 Archaic var. *fei*, predominant (as *fey*) until c. 1840.

[♯19: 9v]

verite per signum Crucis,
Kirie✠Cassiel✠Salmazan
Tetromion Ben Sancta Tri-
nitas Eschretus Christus✠
Tarae Kirie Eleison✠
Ich beschwöre dich Lucifer
und Beelzebub euch beide
Obersten der Teufeln, be-
schwöre euch nochmals ge-
waltig bei dem grosen all-
mächtigen lebendingen, heiligen und einigen Gott, dem
Schöpfer Himmels und der
Erden, ja ich beschwöre euch
bei allen Heiligen Gottes
bei allen heiligen Nahmen

[♯20: 10r]

Gottes, bei allen heiligen
Erzeugeln, daß ihr mir den
Geist N. augenblicklich vor
meinen Kreis zwingst
und bindet und ihm befeh-
let daß er meine Worte
höre, und denselben Folge
leiste, und mir in einer
schönen menschlichen Gestalt
erscheine und meinen Wil-
len und Befehl in allem
vollbringe, und dies feÿ
dir Lucifer und Beelzebub

nebst allen deinem Anhang
geboten bei den Machtwor-
ten Tetragrammaton So-

[#21: 10v]

ther Deus Azetan Hott,
Menean Trensie Zamay,
el Lazamen, Deus Jueba-
tha, Sacraman, Fiat Fiat
Fiat! Das geschehe! Gott feỹ
mir gnädig und barmherzig.
Ihr sollet keine Ruhe haben
vor diesen beiden, sondere
lauter Furcht Fluch und Schrecken soll euch überfallen so-
lange bis ihr ungehorsame
Geister mir gehorsamet und
meinen Willen zu vollbringen
bereit seid. Fiat, Fiat, Fiat
✠✠✠

[#22: 11r]

Dieses ist das Zeichen des
Lucifer und Beelzebub,
denn ein jeder Geist hat
sein eigenes Zeichen.

Nun folget die Citation
Acielis des Schazmeisters[57]

[#23: 11v]

Im Nahmen Gottes des Vat-
ters des Sohnes und des Heiligen Geistes, Amen!

---

57 The writer alternates between *Schatz* and *Schaz*
('treasure'), the latter spelling possibly reflecting the word's
High German etymology, or its persistence in the Central
Franconian dialect area.

Ich N zitire[58] und beschwöre
dich Geist Aciel bei Jesu Christo dem Richter der Lebendigen
und der Todten, durch den
Schöpfer Himmels und der Erden und durch die grosen Nahmen Gottes und hohe Machtworte Jehova Elohim Ado-
nay Agla El Tetragramma-

[#24: 12r]

ton, daß du Geist Aciel
⌐ꝉꞒꝝ in diesem Augen-
blick vor meinem Kreis
erscheinest, und in freundlicher Gestalt in meiner bekann-
ten Sprache mit mir redest,
ohne allen Schauder, Schaden
oder Ungewitter, komm komm
komm!
Ich beschwöre dich Geist Aciel der du bist ein Herr
über alle verborgene Schä-
tze der Erde, bei den kräf-
tigen Worten und Nahmen
Set, Schemhamphoras Du-
gam Dugam Dugam, daß

---

58 Superseded *citiere* (and inflections thereof) c. 1900.

[#25: 12v]

du Geist Aciel diesen verborgenen Schatz, wie er von
Menschen Händen versetzt
worden aus demselbigen Ort
wo er stehet heraus holest
und neben diesen Kreis
legest ohne allen Schrecken
Schauder, Hagel Betrug und
Verblandung und Beschadigung
des Kreises und mein und
meiner Gesellen Leibes und
Seele, dies gebiete ich dir.
Komm! Komm! Komm!
Sacro✠Sancta✠Trinitas✠

Ich gebiete dir Aciel im

[#26: 13r]

Nahmen

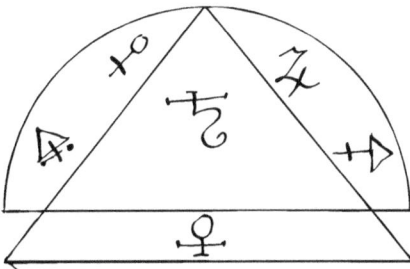

Nisza✠Hagal✠Ligkama

Raphael✠
Komm! Komm! Komm
Fiat! Fiat! Fiat!
Ducam, Ducam, Ducam
Veni! Veni! Veni!
Spiritus Aciel
Signum
Spiritus Aciel.

[#27: 13v]

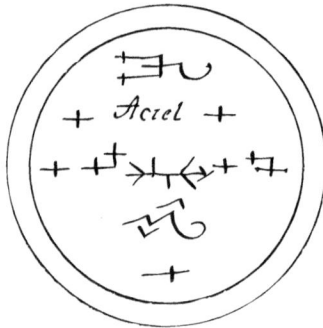

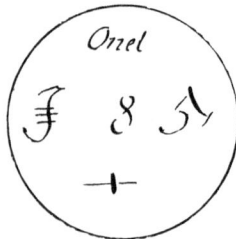

Crucis Christi vincit

[#28: 14r]

He ⚏.

Im Nahmen Gottes des Vat-
ters, des Sohnes und des
Heiligen Geistes.
Ich beschwöre dich mit der
allerheiligsten Dreifaltigkeit, du hochgelobter Engel
der du von Gottes Thron
verstoßen bist, der du be-
schweret mit Tausend See-
len, die du in der Höllen-
pein ausgestoßen hast, und
aus Mutterleibe verschworen
hast, und auch aus des Teu-
fels Gewalt dahin gekom-
men bin, und mich aus

[#29: 14v]

der schweren Last heraus zu-
weissen, Adonai, der ho-
he Prinz Gabriel, der Prinz
Ninive, der Prinz Adonai
unde seine Abgesandten, und
du heiliger Niniverus zu-
sammen gefügt, und das[59]
soll der Teufel nicht scheiden, und das soll der Teufel
nicht scheiden ✠✠✠.
Citation

---

59 Archaic var. *daß*.

eines Stammgeistes.
Stammgeist, der du in diesem Hause (oder Scheuer)
wohnest, ich N. citire dich
im Namen der 14 heiligen

[#30: 15r]

Nothhelfer mit Gottes Kraft
und Macht in Himmel und
auf Erden, und durch die
Kraft und Macht aller heiligen Engel im Himmel, und
durch das Gebet der ganzen
Geistenheit, und die hochheili-
ge dreifaltigkeit dreige und
zwinge dich so lange bis du
mir sichtbarlich in deiner
wirklichen Menschengestalt
erscheinest, und weder Ruhe
noch Rast hast, bis du mir
meinen Willen erfüllest
3. Vatter Unser.
Empfang des Geistes.

[#31: 15v]

Wilkommen seÿ du troziger
Geist, weil du doch driest-
willig bist, ich begehre dich
zusprechen.

Wenn er nun Red[60] und Ant-
wort gibt, dann frage ihn
um seine Umstände ob er
zu erlösen seÿ und womit
er erlöst werden könnte
und zu welcher zeit und
Stund[61] er zu erlösten
wäre. Wann nun die-
ses vorbeÿ[62] ist, so danke
ihn wieder ab und sprich:
Fahre hin im Frieden des
Herrn, der Friede Gottes

[#32: 16r]

welcher höher ist als aller
Menschen Vernunft und al-
ler Geister Verrichtung, seÿ
zwischen mir und dir, wie
eine Feuermauer und Un-
terschied, daß wir nicht zu-
sammen kommen, und du
mir keinen Schaden thun
kannst, das thun ich mir und

---

60 While they may be archaisms, or simply misspellings,
both *Red* (standard German *Rede*) and *Vatter* (*Vater*), above,
could indicate some influence of the Alemannic German
dialect.

61 Another potential Alemannic variant, found with
comparable frequency to the now-standard *Stunde* until c.
1750.

62 Archaic var. *vorbei*, predominant (as *vorbey*) until c. 1805.

dir zur Buß.[63] In nomine
Dei patris et filii et spiritus sancti, Amen!
Diese Abdankung muß 3.
mal gesprochen werden.
Die allerheiligste dreifaltigkeit stehe mir beÿ.

[#33: 16v]

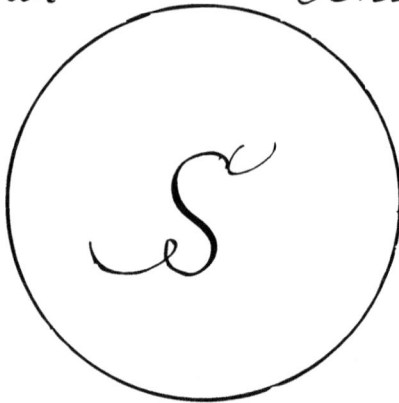

Eloah   *Jehovah*

Ehejeh.

Nun folgen die Nahmen
der heiligen Engel nebst
ihren Planeten Zeichen:

---

63 Archaic var. *Buße*, predominant until c. 1765.

1 ☉ Michael
2 ☽ Gabriel
3 ♂ Samiel
4 ☿ Raphael

[#34: 17r]

5 ♃ Sachiel
6 ♀ Anael
7 ♄ Casiel
Dieses sind die 7 Könige.
Namen
der 7. Obersten.

♑   Aratron — Derdiel
♋   Bethor — Miseriel
♑   Phalig — Seraphiel
♒   Och — Asfariel
8 ♎   Hagith — Salomiel
7 ♒   Ophiel — Sateriel
11 ♏   Pfuel — Jachiel
Folgen 12 Geister mit ihren
Zeichne in welchen sie jeden

[#35: 17v]

Tag der Woche zu berufen
sind.

		Sonntag	Montag	Dinstag	Mittwoch	Donnerstag	Freitag	Samstag
1	Maduth	☉	☽	♂	☿	♃	♀	♄
2	Janor	♀	♄	☉	☽	♂	☿	♃
3	Sullu	☿	♃	♀	♄	☉	☽	♂
4	Nusma	☽	♂	☿	♃	♀	♄	☉
5	Sedethi	♄	☉	☽	♂	☿	♃	♀
6	Thumen	♃	♀	♄	☉	☽	♂	☿
7	Curen	♂	☿	♃	♀	♄	☉	☽
8	Taris	☉	☽	♂	☿	♃	♀	♄
9	Neroa	♀	♄	☉	☽	♂	☿	♃
10	Jaxon	☽	♂	☿	♄	♀	♃	☉
11	Abur	☿	♃	♀	♄	☉	☽	♂
12	Nulbuon	☉	☽	♂	☿	♃	♄	♀

[#36: 18r]

Hierauf werden dir die Geister allen deinen Willen erfüllen und den Schatz übergeben, wann aber die Geister viel Umstände machen wollen, oder sich etwas ausbedingen wollen, so mußt du dich in gar nichts einlassen und ihnen bei Leibe nichts verwilligen, sonst komst du in groses Unglück.

Also hast du nun in diesem
Buch einen sonderbaren Schaz
mein lieber Exorciste, welchen du in Estim und hohen
Ehren zu halten hast, denn

[#37: 18v]

mittelst desselben kanst du
nun die Geister binden und
zwingen und beschworen, daß
sie dir volkommen zu Diensten
seÿn, und dir alles bringen mus-
sen. Vale.
Passau, d. 15te April 1515.

Der schwarze Rabe.

Paſſau,

Anno 1519. ꝟ. 30 July.

Der ſchwarze Rab ſo nicht gebunden
hat ſind den goldnen Ring gefunden
Dab rühe ich mich auch ohne Schand
Daß ich der ſchwarze Rab genannt.

[#6: 3r]

Von der
Einsegnung und Beschwörung
des Zeichens.

Wenn der Leib mit allen
zugehörigen Dingen rein ge-
räucherlich verfertigt ist, von Per-
gament oder Jungfern Pa-
pier, so muß man denselben
einsegnen und beschwören,
alsdenn zwei geweihte Wachs-
kerzen daraus setzen und be-
räuchern, alsdann sprechen:

Im Namen + + + Amen!
Ich N.N. segne und beschwöre
dieses Zeichen bei dem Namen
des großen, gewaltigen und al-

[#7: 3v]

[#8: 4r]

5

ich euch Geister alle in dem Na_
men der allerheiligsten 3.
faltigkeit. Amen.
Ja. za. ri. A + Fla + na _ et
+ Serapſh + Sochliel xe _ se
_ pha + Phasameth + Salma.
sacc + ve. sar + Actu. ar +
Pe. li. ar. so. nor + San. clei.
+ Ja. za. ri. el + La. tri ten
a. za. re. et + Scheliel + Lu.
ri + A. za. mel + Egivi + et
Verchiel + Amuziel + Selo.
el + Eno. di. el + Hamali.
el + Irqueel + Zcaphliel.
+ Osach. y + Na. ma. chay.
+ Na. riel + Haniel + Ra _

[#9: 4v]

6.

phael + O. ri. phi. el.

NB dieſe Worte unterſchei=
de allezeit bey dem +
und geſchiehet jede Sylbe
apart, damit man auch
alles wieder zurück leſen
kann.

[lines of symbols/characters]

Und hiermit beſchwöre ich die
ſen Geiſt bei die Namen Jeſu Chr

[#10: 5r]

[#11: 5v]

8

Wach mit folgendem Gebet
an, und fasse fort mit der
Citation der Geister welchen
die haben willst.

Das nächste Gebet

O, allmächtiger, ewiger,
barmherziger Gott, lieber
himmlischer Vater, der du
die Herzen der Menschen kennst,
weißt und sehr wohl und
ihr Anliegen bestes weißt
als sie dir es sagen können
O, du König aller Könige
und Herr aller Herren und
Regierer der ganzen Welt,
wie deine Kinder bitten

[#12: 6r]

dich demüthiglich mit sanft-
müthigem Geist, du wollest
und gluth Seel und Tugend
gaben, zu diesem unserm
Vorhaben und Werk und uns
zu Hülfe senden, deine heilige Engel, Michael, Gabriel
Samael, Raphael, Sachiel,
Anael und Cassiel, die vor
deinem heiligen Thron ohn
Unterlaß rufen, heilig heilig heilig ist unser Herr
Gott Sabaoth, Himmel und
Erde sind seiner Ehren voll,
sei uns lieber Herr und
Gott und sei uns gnädig

[#43: 6v]

[#14: 7r]

11.

Jesum Christum deinen ein-
gebohrnen allerliebsten Sohn,
d. durch deine heilige Nahmen
Agla, Adonai, Tetragrammaton, Eloah, Sother Emanu-
el, du wollest in diesse
Wörter den Worten meines
Mundes Kraft und Macht
geben, über den bösen En-
gel welcher du von deinem
heiligen Himmel in den
Abgrund verstoßen hast,
daß ich sie möge zwingen
und binden sichtbarlich in
freundlicher Menschen Ge-
stalt vor meinem Kreiß

[#15: 7v]

12

zu erscheinen, und meinen
Worten und Gebot völlig
nachzukommen, bei der heiligen Namen deiner göttli-
chen Majestät Ja + Adonai +
Ara + Auray + Ella + Ama-
len + Essoi + Vision + Ehel +
Heer + Agla + das verleihe
mir o du barmherziger Gott
und lieber Himmlischer Vater, durch Jesum Christum
in Kraft des heiligen Geistes
Amen.

Nun folget die Citation.
Merke daß in dieser Citation
nicht als ein paar Teufel

[#16: 8r]

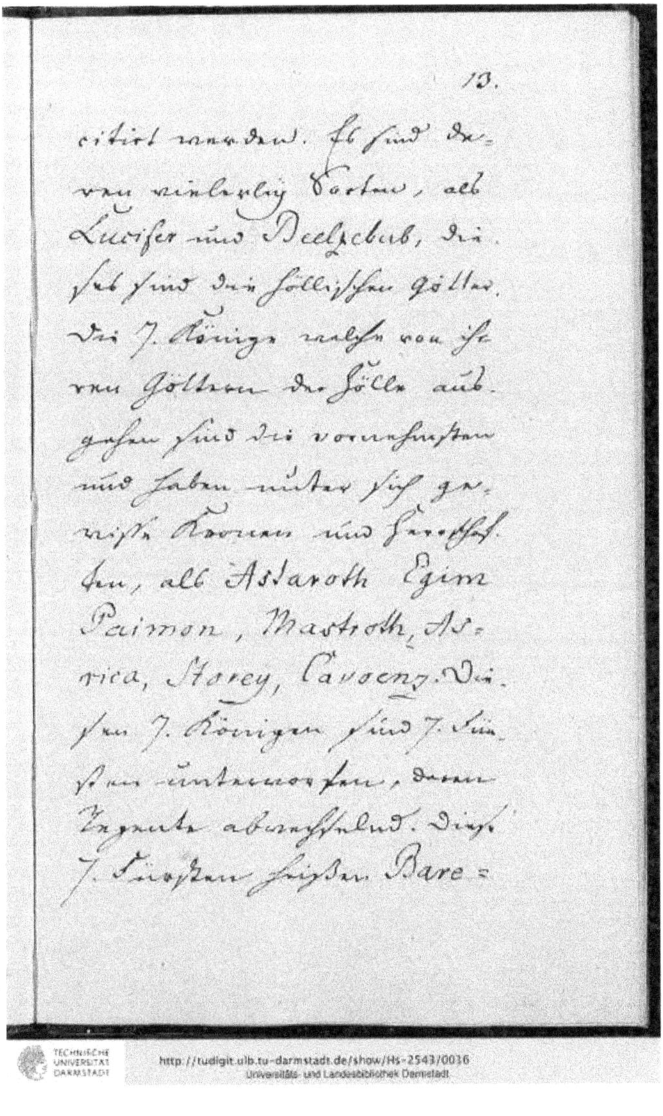

[#17: 8v]

ham, Harthan, Gannax,
Ambuma, Juhbarmon, Ha-
rabejes, Mayston. Diese La-
ben unter sich noch 7 Obri-
Pain, welche sind Nepista,
Shize, Aziabel, Harduel,
Huiquil, Sathiel, Daruel.
    Citation und Be-
        schwörung.
Über die obersten Teufel
Lucifer + Beelzebub + Ray-
mon + Kirie + Emanuel +
EE Eman + Sachriel + Ga-
Palandema + Jehova + Su-
me + Deus + omnes + Spi-
ritus +

[#18: 9r]

15.

Mein Gott, Mein Gott, hilf
mir ℈.

[...] Beelzebub et Lucifer, dugam
dugam.

Ja vac + Lucifer + Rual+
Paymon et omnes Spiritus

[#19: 9v]

16.

venite per signum Crucis,
Kirie + Cassiel + Salmagar
Tetramion Ben Sancta Tri-
nitas Eschratus Christus +
Tarae Kirie Eleison +
Ich beschwöre dich Lucifer
und Beelzebub auch beide
Obersten der Teufeln, be-
schwöre auch nochmall ge-
waltig bei dem großen all-
mächtigen lebendigen hei-
ligen und einigen Gott, den
Schöpfer Himmels und der
Erden, ja ich beschwöre auch
bei allen heiligen Gottes
bei allen heiligen Namen

[#20: 10r]

17

Gottes, bei allen heiligen
Engeln, daß ihr mir den
Geist R. augenblicklich vor
meinen Kreis bringet
und bindet und ihn befeh-
let daß er meine Worte
höre, und denselben Folge
leiste, und mir in einer
schönen menschlichen Gestalt
erscheine und meinen Wil-
len und Befehl in allen
vollbringe, und dieß sey
dir Lucifer und Beelzebub
nebst allen deinen Anhang
geboten bei dem mächtigen
heiligen Tetragrammaton Sa-

[#24: 10v]

18.

ther Deus Azelan Hott,
Menean Trensie Zamay,
el Lazamon, Deus Illeba-
tha, Sacrasman, Fiat Fiat
Fiat! Das geschehe! Gott sey
mir gnädig und barmhertzig.
Ihr sollt kein Leyd haben
vor diesen beiden, sondern
lauter Fürst Flüch und Schor-
ben soll euch überfallen so
lange bis ihr ungehorsame
Geister mir gehorsamt und
meinen Willen zu vollbringen
bereit seyd. Fiat, Fiat, Fiat

+ + +

[#22: 11r]

[#23: 11v]

20.

Im Nahmen Gottes des Vaters und des Sohns und des Heiligen Geistes, Amen!

[magical characters]

Ich Nzitiere und buchstabire dich Geist Aciel bei Jesu Christo dem Richter der Lebendigen und der Todten, durch den Schöpfer Himmels und der Er-den und durch den großen Nah-men Gottes und soll machst Worte Jehova Elohim Ado-nay Agla El Tetragramma

[#24: 12r]

21

ton, daß du Geist Aciel
SHEH in diesem Augen-
blick vor meinem Kreiß
erscheinst, und in freundlicher Gestalt in einer bekann-
ten Sprache mit mir redest,
ohne allen Schauder, Schaden
oder Ungewitter, komm komm
komm!
Ich beschwöre dich Geist Ati-
el daß du bist ein Herr
über alle verborgenen Schä-
tze der Erde, bei den kräf-
tigen Worten und Namen
Jet, Schemhamphoras du
gam dugam dugam, daß

[#25: 12v]

[#26: 13r]

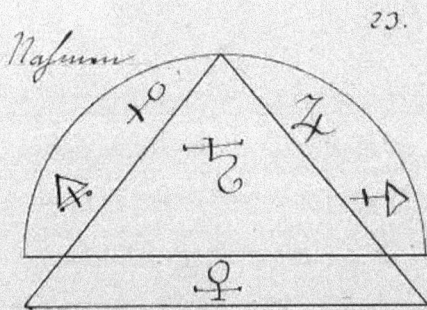

Nisza + Hagal + Zigkama

Raphael +

Komm! Komm! Komm

Fiat! Fiat! Fiat!

Ducam, Ducam, Ducam,

Veni! Veni! Veni!

Spiritus Aciel

Signum

Spiritus Aciel.

[#27: 13v]

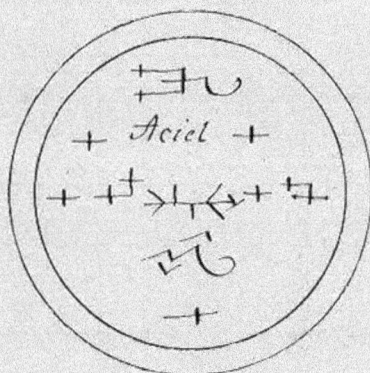

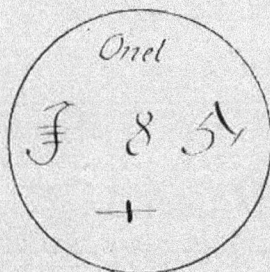

[#28: 14r]

25.

He Z

Im Namen Gottes des Vat.
ters, des Sohnes und des
heiligen Geistes.

Ich beschwöre dich mit der
allerheiligsten Dreifaltigkeit, du Hochgelobter Engel
der du von Gottes Thron
verstoßen bist, der du be-
schwerst mit tausend Pein,
der du in der Höllen-
pein ausgestoßen hast, und
auf Mutterleibe verschworen
hast, und auch aus der Tau-
fe voll Gewalt dahin ge kommen bin, und auch aus

[#29: 14v]

[#30: 15r]

27.

Nothelfer mit Gottes Kraft
und Macht im Himmel und
auf Erden, und durch die
Kraft und Macht aller heiligen Engel im Himmel, und
durch das Gebet der ganzen
Christenheit, und der Hochheili-
gen Dreifaltigkeit zwinge und
zwinge dich so lange biß du
mir sichtbarlich in deiner
wirklichen Menschengestalt
erscheinest, und werde Ruhe
noch Rast haßt, biß du mir
meinen Willen erfüllest
J. Vatter Unser.
Empfang des Geistes.

[#31: 15v]

[#32: 16r]

[#33: 16v]

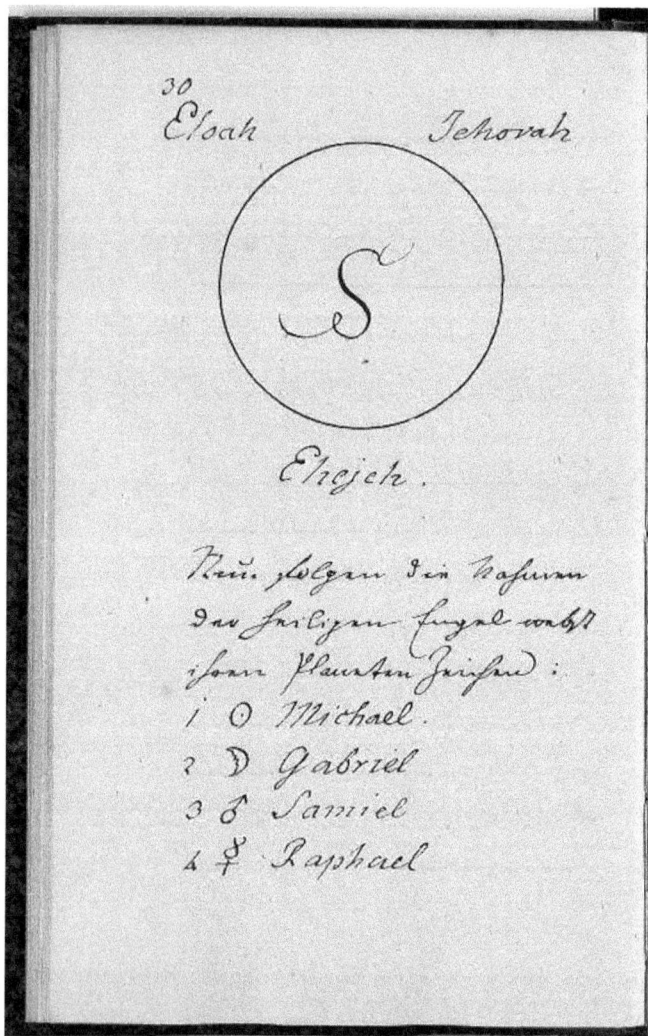

[#34: 17r]

31.

5 ♃ Sachiel
6 ♀ Anael
7 ☿ Casiel

Dieses sind die 7 Könige.

Namen

der 7. Obersten.

♄ Aratron – Derdiel
6♃ Bethor – Miseriel
♐♑ Phaleg – Seraphiel
♂♃ Och – Asfariel
8 △ Hagith – Salomiel
7 ♏ Ophiel Satoriel
11 ♏ Phuel – Jachiel

Folgen 12 Geister mit ihren
Zeichen mit welchen sie jeden

[#35: 17v]

32

Tag der Woch zu brauchen sind.

		Sonntag	Montag	Dienstag	Mittwoch	Donnerstag	Freitag	Samstag
1	Maduth	☉	☽	♂	☿	♃	♀	♄
2	Janor	♀	♄	☉	☽	♂	☿	♃
3	Sullu	☿	♃	♀	♄	☉	☽	♂
4	Nusma	☽	♂	☿	♃	♀	♄	☉
5	Sedothi	♄	☉	☽	♂	☿	♃	♀
6	Thunon	♃	♀	♄	☉	☽	♂	☿
7	Cwen	♂	☿	♃	♀	♄	☉	☽
8	Taris	☉	☽	♂	☿	♃	♀	♄
9	Nersa	♀	♄	☉	☽	♂	☿	♃
10	Jaxon	☽	♂	☿	♄	♀	♃	☉
11	Abur	☿	♃	♀	♄	☉	☽	♂
12	Nulbyon	☉	☽	♂	☿	♃	♄	♀

[#36: 18r]

33

Gewalt werden dir die Geister allen deinen Willen
stellen und den Schatz übergeben, wenn aber die Geister
viel Umstände machen wol-
len, oder sich absolut ausbündi-
gen wollen, so mußt du dich
in gar nicht einlassen und
ihnen bei Leibe nicht einwil-
ligen, sonst kommst du in gro-
ßes Unglück.
Also hast du nun in diesem
Buch einen sonderbaren Schatz
mein lieber Exorciste, weil
hast du in Ostern und höchsten
Ehren zu halten hast, denn

[#37: 18v]

V.

𝕮𝖔𝖓𝖈𝖊𝖗𝖓𝖎𝖓𝖌 𝖉𝖊𝖗 𝕾𝖙𝖆𝖒𝖒𝖌𝖊𝖎𝖘𝖙

A History of Last Things

The Darmstadt manuscript contains a striking selection of seemingly disparate instructions, invocations, and other practical desiderata of the operative conjuror, all of which, however, may conceal a greater unity of purpose than first meets the eye. Of particular note is an exorcistic rite titled "Citation eines Stammgeistes", or "summoning of a haunting spirit".[64] Necromantic operations are certainly not unknown amongst the grimoires and other variegated ephemera of Western ritual magic; from the Mediterranean Sea to the Baltic, practitioners filled their working books with notes on how to get in touch with spirits of the deceased,[65] and literary

---

64 Universitäts- und Landesbibliothek Darmstadt, Hs. 2543, 14v–16r.

65 See for instance the "Experimentum Michaelis Scoti nigromantici" in Biblioteca Medicea Laurenziana, MS plut. 89 sup. 38 (fifteenth century, Italy); "To have the Spirit of a dead body" in British Library, MS Sloane 3851 (seventeenth century, England); and the conjuration of a dead person in the nineteenth-century manuscript from Fru Alstads socken, Skytts härad, Sweden, in Johnson (2019), 588.

evidence like the thirteenth-century *Faereyinga Saga*, wherein the chieftain Þrándr performs a curious rite to summon forth the walking remains of three men in order to discover how they had been killed—one drowned, one decapitated, and the third evidently not worth mentioning, in the event[66]—suggests something of both the native Germanic background and the motives which informed later practices, colored by the advent of Christianity though they may be.

A cursory survey of manuscript and print volumes belonging to the so-called "Faustian" genre[67]—to which, given its provenance and certain aesthetic features, *The Black Raven* may be justifiably ascribed—would seem to indicate that conjuring books of that school, in keeping with their generally magpie-like tendency to accrete secrets and *experimenta* for a great variety of practical purposes (including the often necromancy-adjacent search for buried treasures),[68] regularly included means of adjuring the restless dead. The Darmstadt text has close company in this respect: though much more elaborated than the characteristically succinct instructions given in the *Raven*, a parallel sort of working appears in one of the several compendia bearing a title evoking the "natural and unnatural

---

66 "The Saga of Thrond of Gate", XL.

67 Operations of a more or less evidently necromantic nature appear in Herzogin Anna Amalia Bibliothek F 4348, F 8476, and Hs. Q 455[b]. This is certainly not a defining feature of the Faustian oeuvre, however: cf. HAAB, Hs. Q 455.

68 Henning and Paisey (1978), 5–6.

magic of Doctor Johannes Faust".[69] In volume 3 of this sprawling *Miracul-Kunst und Wunderbuch* we find a chapter title that appears to more explicitly confirm the specific nature of the "haunting" or "lingering" spirits being addressed in this type of operation, namely "Stammgeistern derer verstorbenen Menschen", that is, "of deceased persons".[70] Also of note is a Latin conjuration attributed to Saint Cyprian, included as an appendix to the *Verus Jesuitarum Libellus* collected by Johann Scheible alongside numerous more explicitly Faustian texts, whereby a person's ghost is adjured to render up a treasure they had buried *in vita*.[71]

A literature of conjurations and exorcisms of the dead implies a very well developed, if rather fluid, set of eschatological conceptions. Of course, beliefs about the spirits of persons lingering after death to haunt milieux pertinent to the routines of their former life, or to the circumstances of its end, can be found circulating long before the early modern period with its profusion of publications both occult and vulgar. The Roman playwright Plautus (third–second century BCE), in his comic *Mostellaria*, has a crafty servant convince his master's father that his house is haunted by the victim

---

69 HAAB, Hs. Q 455[b], *D. Iohannis Faustii Magia Naturalis Et Innaturalis; oder unerforschlicher Höllen-Zwang/ das ist Miracul-Kunst u. Wunderbuch wodurch ich die Höllischen Geister habe bezwungen/ daß sie in allen meinen Willen vollbringen haben müßten.* Cf. *Doktor Johannes Faust's Magia Naturalis et Innaturalis: oder, Dreifacher Höllenzwang, Letztes Testament und Siegelkunst* [...] *in fünf Abtheilungen*, Scheible (1849).

70 HAAB, Hs. Q 455[b], vol. 3: 11.

71 Scheible (1846), 846–851.

of a long-past murder, and Ptolemaic Egypt gives us the tale of Setne Khamwas and Naneferkaptah, wherein another tragically deceased ghost stands guard over a forbidden treasure in his Memphite tomb—a book of magical spells,[72] as it happens, which, as any treasure-hunting magician of a later era would attest, was often worth more than its weight in gold.[73] The ghostly custodianship of hidden valuables, as well as the disquiet of those who meet bad ends, will go on to become perennial motifs of ghostlore.

As the ghost stories of pagan antiquity were displaced (and in some cases, shamelessly reappropriated) by those of the Christian era,[74] the question naturally arose: on what basis could adherents of this new theology—which at least notionally placed every person's final disposition definitively beyond the terrestrial plane—entertain a belief that the souls of the dead might remain somehow accessible to the living, and even continue to linger upon the earth? Some of the Church Fathers allowed that the sanctified dead may respond to the entreaties of the living, albeit only by the dispensation of divine providence, and not through any inherent power of their own.[75] While intercession by the saints was, and would remain, a contentious issue,[76] in medieval Western Europe the doctrine of Purgatory gradually came to provide conceptual legitimation for

---

72 Lichtheim (1980), 125 ff.

73 Dillinger (2012), 93.

74 O'Lynn (2018), 135–6.

75 Bartlett (2013), 104.

76 Bartlett (2013), 588–96.

the virtually ubiquitous human experience of revenance by the recently deceased, irrespective of their imputed blessedness.[77] At the very cusp of the period commonly delineated as the "Middle Ages", the Venerable Bede defined Purgatory as the state of those who, although "preordained to the lot of the elect on account of their good works", were yet "chastised, and...seized by the flames of the fire of purgatory" after death, due to some transgression which had rendered them insufficiently pure to enter Paradise. They would endure this cleansing fire until Judgment Day, unless "the petitions, almsgiving, fasting, weeping, and oblation of the saving sacrificial offering by their faithful friends" should win them absolution sooner.[78] The salvific role of suffrages performed by the living on behalf of the dead was a major point of emphasis in many late medieval ghost tales of a homiletic nature.[79] Presumably even more effective than the prayers of the laity, an official pardon from ordained clergy might be invoked in emergency situations; a twelfth-century account from William of Newburgh relates how a man rose from the grave to terrorize the people of Buckinghamshire until Bishop Hugh of Lincoln sent a letter of absolution to be placed upon the breast of the corpse as he lay in his tomb.[80] Narratives such as this also implicitly reinforced the assumption that revenant phenomena were in fact prompted in some way by the soul or personality of

---

77 Marshall (2002), 234.

78 Bede, *Homilies on the Gospels*, in Moreira (2010), 17.

79 McKeever (2010), 65–6.

80 Simpson (2003), 390–2.

the deceased, and not, as in certain competing theories with which these stories were contemporary, some form of demonic trickery or possession.

That the penitential stasis of the dead could be located spatially within the material world had been proposed as early as the *Dialogues* of Gregory the Great in the sixth century.[81] Gregory's tales, intended for the theological and moral edification of Christendom, proved sufficiently colorful to enjoy a popular readership well into the Middle Ages and beyond, and their conceit regarding earthly Purgatories would be reflected in literature both popular and learned; the most widely-read work of the fifteenth-century Carthusian Jacob of Jüterbog was his 1454 *De apparitionibus animarum post exitum*, a systematic examination of ghostly phenomena written at the behest of some Leipzig Franciscans looking for a solution to the haunting of their friary,[82] and Heinrich Cornelius Agrippa could still adduce a contemporary belief (at least among those willing to countenance the practice of necromancy) in certain places being fit for terrestrial purgation in his 1533 *De Occulta Philosophia*.[83]

Conversely, the Church was not oblivious to the value of ghost phenomena as evidence of Purgatory's reality, and of the efficacy of liturgical means by which souls could be released from it.[84] Indeed, the funeral Mass—over which the ecclesiastical

---

81 Moreira (2010), 85–9.

82 Koslofsky (2000), 26.

83 Agrippa, III.42.

84 O'Lynn (2018), 58.

authorities exercised a monopoly—was regarded as the most powerful and efficacious suffrage by means of which a soul might be hastened from Purgatory to its final heavenly reward,[85] a notion which practicing necromancers did not shy away from wielding in their negotiations with recalcitrant shades, as we shall see. Both before and following the Protestant Reformation, ghosts were often purported to seek mortal intercession of one kind or another in order to right whatever wrong had condemned them to a grim unlife.[86] In some cases, such as the collection of late fourteenth-century tales from Byland Abbey, the penitent dead were understood to be cursed with a certain passivity in this regard, only able to divulge the reason for their wandering if specifically asked by one of the living[87]—an idea perhaps reflected in the scripts of exorcistic texts like the *Raven*, which stipulate what one must inquire of a spectre once it has been conjured to appear. Whether or not explicit reference was made to the doctrine of Purgatory, it was only by first revealing the crime to which a soul's fate was bound, by exposing to public knowledge a guilty party's culpability, that amelioration could be effected, in this world as well as the next. In this way, a ghostly sending might amount to a second chance at the public confession and penance of which the deceased failed to

---

85 Koslofsky (2000), 23.

86 McKeever (2010), 7–8.

87 Simpson (2003), 395.

avail themself in life.[88]

Martin Luther's decisive repudiation of purgatorial doctrine with his 1530 *Widerruf vom Fegefeuer* (Repeal of Purgatory)[89] was by no means the first rumbling of dissent toward the idea. Nearly a century prior, the Bohemian reformer Petr Chelčický was denying the reality of Purgatory as a metaphysical state, as well as the efficacy of mortal acts of intercessory atonement.[90] Catholics and Protestants continued to exchange polemics on the question well into the seventeenth century, with Jesuit authors propounding the positive Catholic position which tended to make Purgatory a vivid and material place, and its punishments embodied and specific— the very notions that Protestants found most absurd.[91] At the same time, the Counter-Reformation saw its own anti-superstitionist reaction against unregulated commerce with souls, the 1586 papal bull *Coeli et terrae*

---

88 See *Great news from Middle-Row in Holbourn, or, A true relation of a dreadful ghost which appeared in the shape of one Mrs. Adkins...on Tuesday-night last, being the 16th of this instant March, 1679*, for one object lesson in the ways "that Murther bears a lasting stain and clogs the Conscience of the Guilty Soul with the restless fears and jelosies which often make despairing Mortals unaccused by Man, betray them selves, or if not so, at least when Death, has closed their Eyes, and as the World imagines, they repose in a long slumber, till the dreadful day of rendring Account, their restless Spirits forced about the Earth, do wander up and down until they have made known those Crimes the Party represented in those thin and Airy forms did in their Lifetimes act".

89 Marshall (2002), 48.

90 Maly (2015), 247.

91 Maly (2015), 258–60.

categorically proscribing all forms of divination and magic, including necromancy as well as its affiliated practice of treasure hunting.[92] Officials like Bishop Otto Truchseß von Waldburg, who oversaw the exorcism of an alleged ghost in the household of the Fugger banking family in 1568, sought to place limits on the freedom with which souls in Purgatory were popularly supposed to communicate with the living, tending to insist—despite a theoretical place for such phenomena within orthodoxy—that they represented diabolic manipulations rather than entreaties by the penitent dead seeking intercession;[93] the provenance of such apparitions was, after all, discouragingly opaque, and human discernment fallible. The Jesuit order worked in concert with civil authorities to inculcate the officially approved post-Tridentine demonology and eschatology in the Catholic territories of the Holy Roman Empire,[94] and in 1612 the Bavarian *Landgebott wider die Aberglauben, Zauberey, Hexerey und andere sträffliche Teufelskünste* enshrined the injunctions of *Coeli et terrae* in secular law, criminalizing all forms of unlicensed discourse with spirits, including exorcism.[95]

Nevertheless, the irrefutable phenomenology of revenant apparitions demanded reconciliation with the new reformed orthodoxies. Protestantism sought to resolve this discrepancy through the demonological solution of Ludwig Lavater and others, which identified

---

92 Lederer (2002), 28; Tarrant (2020), 46–7.

93 Lederer (2002), 31–4; Ferber (2002), 64–6.

94 Lederer (2002), 28–9.

95 Lederer (2002), 34–5.

supposed ghosts of the deceased as, in fact, lying devils.[96] Despite the theologians' best efforts, however, the dead continued to have a very real and interactive presence among the living. In post-Reformation Württemberg it remained customary to pray for the wellbeing of a soul during the forty days it was believed to linger on earth after death; conversely, failure to bless the deceased with an appropriate benediction left the spirit open to coercive necromantic questioning by malicious neighbors.[97] In the 1640s, Rosina Blökhl-Huber, having successfully defended the licitness of her ghost-laying practices under Inquisitorial torture, became something of a celebrity exorcist to the elites of still-Catholic Bavaria, resolving numerous hauntings where the vigils and aspersions of the clergy had failed, simply by asking the spirits who they were, and what they required.[98] A number of ghost legends from the English West Midlands, recorded in the late nineteenth and early twentieth century, despite treating the subject in a highly demonized manner—with spirits manifesting in horrific bestial forms, their exorcists adjuring them into snuff boxes and disposing of them in some watery abyss—retain the basic assumption that what is being

---

96 Edwards (2012), 355.

97 Scribner (2001), 294–5.

98 Lederer (2002), 41–5.

dealt with is the soul of a specific deceased individual.[99]
According to seventeenth-century Scottish folklorist
Robert Kirk, the highlanders

> ...affirme those Creatures that move invisibly
> in a House, and cast hug great Stones...to
> be Souls that have not attained their Rest,
> thorough[*sic*] a vehement Desire of revealling a
> Murther or notable Injurie done or received,
> or a Treasure that was forgot in their Liftyme
> on Earth, which when disclos'd to a Conjurer
> alone, the Ghost quite removes.[100]

Notably, it was first of all to a "conjurer", rather
than a cleric, that Kirk's informants would expect to
turn in case of a troublesome spectre. Given the deeply
divided and somewhat chaotic state of confessional
relations in late seventeenth-century Scotland, the
average highlander—more likely than the populace at
large to be a Catholic holdout—may well have been

---

99 Simpson (2003), 398. The conjuration of a spirit into a
snuff box or other mundane receptacle could conceivably be
an allusion to the idea that King Solomon once did likewise,
a notion folklorically associated with the king since perhaps
the first century CE or before (see Duling, Testament of
Solomon xvi.6), and echoed in the seventeenth-century
English *Lemegeton*, where he is said to have trapped a horde
of demons in a vessel of brass. Casting troublesome spirits
into a body of water is, of course, recommended by the
Gospel account of the Gerasene demoniac. Interestingly,
both of these elements recur in ghost tales of Germany as
well; see Hubert (2022), 197, 214.

100 Kirk (1893), 23–4.

ambivalent about approaching their local church official. It may also not be insignificant that, in similar early modern Scottish contexts, the familiar spirits which conjurers or cunning folk regularly employed were themselves sometimes understood to be the souls of the dead, or at least to appear in the form of such.[101] Likewise, Mary Parish, a London cunning woman who came into the orbit of chronically impecunious aristocrat Goodwin Wharton in the 1680s, professed to keep the ghost of a man named George Whitmore, whom she had met during their mutual internment at Ludgate prison prior to George's execution, as a confidant and informant.[102]

Even in such staunchly Protestant lands, accounts persisted of ghosts returning to complain of an undelivered message, unredeemed property, or other unfinished business. In 1691, John Dyer of Southwark, London, was troubled by the nocturnal clamor and apparition of his recently-dead wife, "it is thought, because her Husband had lent Money without her consent, which she feared would be lost". The Dyers may have had outstanding debts of their own, for she also "bid him go to Barnaby-street, and fetch Fifteen Pounds, and pay it to Mr. Mealing the Brewer".[103] In 1637, Elizabeth Leakey of Somerset claimed to have been harassed by the spirit of her deceased mother-in-law, until she inquired of the apparition whether there was "any thing left undone in your will that I can doe for

---

101 Wilby (2005), 18, 69.

102 Clark (1984), 27–8.

103 *A true relation of the dreadful ghost appearing to one John Dyer.*

you?" and learned that the ghost required the delivery of an outstanding bond, retrieval of her son's valuables from another daughter-in-law, and conveyance of a confidential message to her own daughter in Ireland.[104] The post-mortem appeals of relatives frequently seem to embody (and, if heeded, provide the means of defusing) inter- and intra-familial tensions which the deceased was unable to resolve—and for which they may have been responsible—in life. Perhaps it was for this reason that an Anglican theologian like Henry More saw value in moderating his peers' demonization or outright denial of such encounters, arguing instead that the traditional dynastic concerns of inheritance, compensatory justice, and admonishment of one's heirs were entirely plausible motives for intervention by the dearly departed, and not at all suggestive of anything diabolic.[105] Accounts of the revenant dead could also be conveniently cited in order to refute materialist arguments against the immortality of the soul.[106]

Outside the rarefied circles of elite discourse, the harbingering ghost remained a fixture of popular literature and drama throughout the early modern period, in both Catholic and Protestant territories.[107] At the same time, popular Catholic devotional literature circulated widely, disseminating a perspective that emphasized ongoing communication and mutual

104 Marshall (2002), 259-60.
105 Marshall (2002), 263.
106 McKeever (2010), 182–4.
107 Edwards (2012), 356.

aid between the living and the dead.[108] Gutenberg's press may well have provided one vector by which the traditional eschatology continued to permeate Protestant consciousness, notwithstanding the official gatekeepers of confessional boundaries. The occult sciences, too, may have furnished a medium free from explicit denominational biases for the diffusion of ideas about ghosts. Agrippa's contention that the souls of the dead may be magically called up "in places where these kinds of souls are known to be most situated, either because of some affinity, as if their abandoned body was drawing them because of some affection once imprinted in their life drawing the soul to some place" (or in those gloomy locales most apt for purgatorial penance)[109] parallels the popular literature produced for the edification of early modern Protestants, in which the untimely deceased most typically haunted— or at least pointed their still-living proxies (often friends and family) toward—the place of their demise, or the person by whom they had been slain, or the site bearing evidence of their own misdeed.[110] Similarly, the neoplatonist astrologer and occult philosopher John Heydon, in his treatise on *The Harmony of the World*, averred that the disembodied soul or *genius*, in its aerial medium, retained the faculties of sense by which it might perceive the material world and its goings-on,[111] and so too an intellect and will in conformity with

---

108 Maly (2015), 264–6.

109 Agrippa, *loc. cit.*

110 McKeever (2010), 253–4.

111 Heydon (1662), 182–3.

what it possessed in life, such that "the *Souls* of men departed, though they have put off, with the body, the capacity of ordinary functions of humane life; yet they may assist and abet them, as pursuing some designe in them".[112] The lingering dead, then, whether beatified intercessor or vexed mother-in-law, were quite ready to intervene in the affairs of the living, if and when it suited their own vicarious aims.[113]

As noted above, methods by which to facilitate the post-mortem departure of a troubled (and perhaps trouble-making) individual have been a perennial feature of magical specialists' repertoires, and became no less so despite countervailing developments in the prevailing eschatological orthodoxy. Despite doctrinal revisions imposed by the Protestant Reformation, and longstanding official disapprobation in general, the pursuit of discourse with the dead in order to glean the particular sorts of intelligence they were popularly imputed to possess never entirely abated.[114] That intelligence most naturally pertained to the condition of the ghost itself, namely the circumstances which had led it to remain lingering on earth. Such contingencies were typically of the sort we have already seen the dead so eager to disclose—an unjust death, an unresolved crime committed by or against the individual in life, pending financial transactions, or simply an accumulation of

112 Heydon (1662), 191.

113 At least until, following many an age of metempsychotic distillation, they "change their *Aerial Vehicle* for an *Ætherial one*", and remain thereafter permanently in the orbit of God; Heydon, 241–2.

114 Harms (2019), 63–4.

spiritual transgressions which demanded some term of purgatorial penance before departing to its final reward. The fact that some of these details could provide an exorcist the opportunity for material remuneration did not go unnoticed.

The 1675 account of a haunted house near Northamptonshire[115] contains several elements which seem to typify not only popular ideas about the etiology of such revenants, but also about the likely manifestations of (and requisite protocols for) spirit apparitions in general. The homeowners, one goodman Clark and family, had been terrorized by poltergeist activity for upwards of a year until, finding himself one day confronted by the ghost, Clark took it upon himself to interrogate the spirit in a manner, *mutatis mutandis*, not dissimilar to that we find prescribed in the *Raven* and similar manuals of conjuration. The ghost initially appears "in a very horrid...shape", but when Clark "took the courage; (In the Name of Almighty God, blessed for ever,) to Demand *what it was*, and *what it would have*?" the ghost immediately assumed "a more familiar and humane shape....with a pleasant friendly countenance, and distinct voice". The invocation of divine names is standard exorcistic practice, taken up in magical contexts from the earliest times,[116] and remained current well into the age of the early modern grimoires for purposes of compelling cooperation from spirits, whether these were construed as ex-carnate in

---

115 *The Rest-less ghost* (1675).

116 See Scurlock (1988) for examples from Neo-Assyrian Mesopotamia.

nature, or something more ambiguous.[117] Likewise, the stipulations to appear in a form and manner more or less human and free of anything *unheimlich*, and to communicate in a clear voice and without dissimulation, are commonplace in these same sources, and indeed we see the *Raven* conjuring its haunt "by the strength and power of God in Heaven and on Earth" to "appear to me visibly in your true human form".

Once Clark had gotten the man's ghost to behave in a civil manner, the spirit related to him a story that could have been taken straight from the mouth of Plautus's own fictional spectre:

> I am the disturbed Spirit of a person long since Dead, I was Murthered neer this place Two hundred sixty and seven years, nine weeks, and two days ago, to this very time, and come along with me and I will shew you where it was done.

The spirit went on to explain that he had left behind a cache of gold and some documents, buried at his former home in Southwark, London, "and that till the same was taken up and disposed of according to his mind, he should never be at rest." Clark agrees to assist

---

117 Instances of the former appear in the seventeenth-century British Library, MS Sloane 3851; see Rankine (2011), 235 ff. Examples of the latter are ubiquitous, the sixteenth-century Folger Library, MS V.b.26 being representative; see Harms, Clark, and Peterson (2015), passim.

the ghost in this matter,[118] and ultimately everyone lives happily ever after, the gold perhaps distributed amongst the present inhabitants of the house (whom the ghost had identified as his "posterity"), and the spirit "henceforth...at rest, so as never more to trouble thee." English magical manuscripts of the early modern period contained rituals precisely—among many other purposes—for compelling spirits to divulge information of the sort related by the Northamptonshire ghost, so that the exorcist might intervene to somehow reduce their suffering,[119] and the *Raven* appears to suggest that the German cultural context was little different in this regard, instructing the conjuror to ask their wraithly interlocutor "if he would be released from his circumstances, and by what means he may be set free, and at what time and hour he would be put at liberty". Interestingly, when Clark asks the ghost why he had not brought his plight to anyone's attention sooner, the spirit replies that he had attempted to do so for several years after his murder, "but was at last laid, and bound down by the Magical Art of a certain Fryer...for some two hundred and fifty [years], during which time he

118 It is worth noting that Clark proceeded with this course of action under the unanimous advice of his parish minister and "several other learned and Godly men", who, nonetheless, warned him "not to eat or drink in any place whether [the ghost] should lead him". A comparison with the myth of Persephone and Hades is unavoidable, and it is not unlikely that this staple of the classical tradition suggested to the educated men of Northamptonshire an implicit caveat against accepting the hospitality of one's cthonic host.

119 Harms (2019), 66. See for example MS Sloane 3851, *The Grimoire of Arthur Gauntlet.*

was confined from appearing on earth".[120] Needless to say, this would seem to reflect a rather irresponsible lack of pastoral care on the part of that particular mendicant-magician, though very much the same attitude evinced by those callously Protestant exorcists of the West Midlands mentioned above, and perhaps the sort of workmanlike expediency to be expected of a freelance clerical necromancer.

Certain tropes of ghost laying seem to have enjoyed a broad geographic dissemination, with many local legends from the South West of England sharing etiological elements with some of the accounts mentioned above. Similar to the West Midlands exorcisms, ghosts from those counties on the Bristol Channel were often banished to a marsh, riverine pool, or other remote body of water. Likewise current was the idea of first compelling the spirit into a receptacle before disposing of it; the ghost of a man named Lucott from North Somerset was ushered by a vicar to the Doniford coast, where he was placed in a little box and unceremoniously thrown into the sea.[121] Again, like the Northamptonshire ghost, these tales also frequently emphasize the temporary nature of a ghost's dismissal, perhaps a dim recollection of the transitory interim of Purgatory to which marginal souls were committed in

---

120 A near contemporary account from St. Sepulchre's, London, 1680, likewise revolves around a cache of money left behind following a murder, with the ensuing poltergeist activity temporarily suppressed, albeit only for a dozen years in this instance (*A Most strange and dreadful apparition of several spirits & visions*).

121 Brown (1979), 28–9.

an earlier age. The revenant of Robert Fry of Mebury, Devon, and that of a Squire Fulford of Dunsford, were each laid to rest where frequent floodwaters should have kept them bogged down, but the presiding clerics warned their respective households that the ghosts would nonetheless make their way home at a pace of "one cockstride" each year, or even each night.[122] In an early nineteenth-century case from Salcombe Regis, one Mr. Lyde returned to haunt his house until, having been unsuccessfully conjured by a number of ministers (in some accounts said to have been called in from Cambridge), he was finally laid for either fifty or sixty years by an Oxford clerk.[123] Out of sight they may have been, but if the persistence of such legends— some for hundreds of years after their putative date of occurrence—is any indication, expelling the ghost of an unpleasant or socially problematic person was not enough to dispel their memory.

Profitable Familiars

If the abolition of Purgatory could result in the spirits of the fretful dead being treated no better than devils—a theological inconvenience to be conjured into a box—the alternative notion, that a ritual technician could shortcut a soul's divinely-ordained purgation, still implied a certain degree of leverage on the part of

122 Brown (1979), 24–5.

123 Brown (1979), 26–7. An odd reflection of the old university rivalry, given the setting's lack of geographic proximity to either school.

the exorcist, and contemporary textual evidence seems to imply that no few freelance *psuchagogoi* drew that same conclusion. Indeed, answering the necromancer's queries (for the ostensible purpose of relating how they might take intercessory action on the spirit's behalf) was just one among various conditions of service that might be imposed upon such a shade under the catch-all clause "fulfill my will".

An iconic example (coming, admittedly, from the pen of a hostile polemicist) appears in Reginald Scot's 1584 *Discoverie of Witchcraft*. This ritual actually entailed approaching a man bound for the executioner's gibbet and compacting for his pending ghostly servitude *before* his death, in return for which the magician swears to give alms and pray for the man's soul throughout the remainder of his own lifetime (presumably to defray the sins that had led to the compactee's execution in the first place).[124] This appears to be very much like the method by which Mary Parish secured the eternal companionship of her friend George. Perhaps tellingly, the chapters immediately following in Scot contain additional *vinculi* and conjurations, suggesting that the mere word of a living soul may not remain sufficiently binding once it had shuffled off the mortal coil. An experiment which closely parallels the one adduced by Scot was recorded around the same time in the

---

124 Scot, XV.xvii. The additional operation appended to the 1665 edition (XV.ii), whereby to interrogate one dead by suicide, also makes provision to ask the spirit "by what means the Magitian may assist it to come to rest" and "to use what means can possibly be used for the procuring rest unto the Spirit."

"boke which is callyd the Dannel".[125] In this case, the pre-mortem individual with whom one negotiates is terminally ill, rather than a condemned criminal, and he is contracted specifically to fetch one "an other spryte which is a corier" who will, together with the deceased, procure a "boke of all sprytes names both in the ayre and in the earth", consecrated by the authority of the ".4. kynges of the elamentes". A consecrated *liber invocationum* by which to call and bind spirits could be a powerful aid, if not a *sine qua non*, to successful exorcism, and methods for obtaining one—either by one's own resources or through a supernatural agent—have been recommended since at least the late medieval period.[126] The ghost's cooperation in this enterprise is secured by "his trewthe and his Crystendome" (i.e. his personal pledge, along with the very baptism by which he was reborn in Christ, which is returned to him at the wet end of a basil wand upon the pact's conclusion), pledged to the magician in return for a promise to look into "how he farthe, and what wyll helpe hym" in his liminal state, and that any pending "matteres shalbe fulfellyd". In other words, the same eschatological anxieties which under other circumstances might prompt a haunting, are here proactively called into play as necromantic bargaining chips.

---

125 Edited by Janneke Stam (2016); see in particular pp. 57–64.

126 See, e.g., the fifteenth-century Bayerische Staatsbibliothek, MS Clm 849, 52r–59v, 135r–139r; the late sixteenth-century British Library, MS Harley 2267, 19v–26r; and the aforementioned means "To have the Spirit of a dead body" in British Library, MS Sloane 3851.

However, if the living could not be counted on to keep faith with their local necromancer once they had passed the veil of death, neither was the still-living necromancer explicitly bound to hold up their own end of the bargain. One ritual in MS Sloane 3851 promises "five Masses on the holy feast of blessed Mary the virgin for forgiveness and pardon of thy Soul from year to year while I live" in return for a spirit's obedient service, but the otherwise meticulous instructions make no further mention of actually fulfilling this obligation.[127] Nonetheless, it was perhaps only through the living that the unquiet dead could hope to escape their liminal state. As Aidan O'Lynn observes, earth-bound souls found themselves in that unenviable condition due to their own lack of Christian charity in life, and it was only through the *caritas* of the living that they might transcend it.[128]

While this liberation was notionally to be effected through theologically-approved forms of intercession such as prayer and indulgences,[129] ghosts sometimes required more unorthodox means of assistance, in which pious concern for the state of a soul could overlap with a magician's entrepreneurial self-interest. We have already seen more than one example of a ghost troubled by undisclosed funds, and resolving the final disposition of an earthly treasure was among the most

---

127 David Rankine, in his edition of the text, notes that the extant manuscript may be incomplete at this point; Rankine (2011), 236.

128 O'Lynn (2018), 61.

129 See Marshall (2002), 18 ff.

frequently cited forms of unfinished business keeping souls from passing on to the next world—so frequent, in fact, that Shakespeare could have Horatio state it as a commonplace.[130] By the same token, eager treasure-hunters could readily interpret a ghostly manifestation as probable evidence of concealed riches in its vicinity, to be subsequently confirmed by interrogating the historical record embodied in still-living local memory, as well as more occult forms of divination.[131] Well into the nineteenth century, treasure hunters sought to rouse the multitudes of dead occasioned by the Thirty Years' War in hopes of retrieving the wealth they had no doubt stashed away, hidden from roving soldiers and other bandits,[132] and the popular correlation of ghosts with treasure was such in seventeenth-century Württemberg that a haunting might be cited as legal evidence to execute a search warrant.[133] It was then a simple matter of putting spade to soil and relieving the deceased of their karmic anchor.

Treasure hunters across seventeenth- and eighteenth-century Germany could thus argue in utmost good faith that availing themselves of the secreted caches of wealth they recovered was an act of charity. In one contemporary example, the text of a thaumaturgical prayer from a Bavarian *Schatz Büchel* (little treasure book) begs God's grace "to receive this treasure, for the benefit of myself and all

---

130 *Hamlet* I.1.148–50.

131 O'Lynn (2018), 141–2.

132 Lederer (2002), 47.

133 Dillinger (2012), 74.

Christendom and for the consolation and peace of the poor souls, now buried".[134] After all, the treasures' original owners were clearly culpable for the sin of avarice, if not theft or deception as well, and therefore found their own redemption bound up with that of their property;[135] putting those goods in the hands of someone who could still make use of them, albeit ever so arbitrarily, rectified a natural order—of life and death, of the migration of the soul, as well as that of inheritance and the circulation of capital. Indeed, an invocation in the seventeenth-century Sloane MS 3824 makes this quite explicit, calling upon the spirits to yield up hidden treasure "to the Sons of Men for whose use it was principally & primarily decreed and ordained",[136] and "that has been the Manufacturison [sic] of Men, & heretofore in use among them, buried in the Earth, or otherwise laid up & hidden... And so thereby said to be corrupted of them & amongst them, whereby Posterity is denied, the benefit of, & comfort thereof".[137] Johannes Dillinger argues that the pious motives of (at least some) treasure hunters contributed to the popular idea that access to secreted valuables was often barred by the minions of Hell. If liberating a hoard of gold could facilitate the liberation of its former owner's soul, then the Devil would be at pains

---

134 Herzog August Bibliothek Wolfenbuttel, Cod. Guelf. 648 Novi, in Lederer (2002), 48–9.

135 Dillinger, Feld (2002), 166–8.

136 Rankine (2009), 32.

137 Ibid., 33.

to keep that money in the ground.[138] This presumed antagonism between diabolic spirits and mortal souls bound to the treasure caches over which those demons stand guard is sometimes played out explicitly in the text of early modern magical treasure-hunting manuals, such as the so-called *Pneumatologia occulta et vera* (possibly dating to the seventeenth or eighteenth century, but printed in an edition by Georg Conrad Horst in the 1820s), wherein the exorcist is warned that the wicked spirits will begin threatening and torturing such a ghost virtually from the outset of the treasure-retrieval conjuration, and must be compelled to obedience with extensive prayers, incantations, and suffumigations.[139] Conversely, another experiment from Sloane MS 3824, perhaps reflecting the influence of the English Reformation more thoroughly than some of the other instances we've discussed, appears to offer an alternative explanation for supernatural phenomena surrounding households that bear a tragic history (and possibly concealed treasure), namely that "for the wickedness of Some person or family, the Good Angels Curses [sic] Such a person, family or House, then the Evil Spirits have power given them, to execute the justice & Decree of the most high God... then Doth the Aerial Spirit haunt, infest & trouble Such houses or places... neither Shall Such house or inhabitant be as Quiet nor shall any of the Generation of any Such family prosper, until providence be appeased, the

138 Dillinger (2012), 79.

139 Horst (1821), 82: "... so werden die böße Geister alsdann die arme Seel äußerst bedrohen und quälen, damit sie sich der Beschwörung widersetzen solle."

Curse Expiated, and the Angry Angel or Aerial Spirit Discharged, or the enchantment taken off from the Treasure, if any be there hid, & the spirit Keeping it be Discharged therefrom, & Cast out, Sent away to his place of residence, otherwise appointed & Decreed for him"[140]—not dissimilar from many narratives of a poltergeist in need of laying, albeit eliminating any role for a deceased person *per se* in the expiation process.

Given these considerations, it is perhaps no surprise to find the summons of a haunting spirit juxtaposed with one pertaining to the spirit Aciel, "the master of treasures", in the *Raven*. After all, once one's ghostly parolee has indicated the location of the trove keeping them bound in limbo, there is still the matter of retrieving it from beneath the earth; constraining the "lord over all hidden treasures" to fetch it out and lay it beside one's consecrated circle bypasses the onerous task of digging, while also averting any demonic or magical traps which may have been laid to deter just such an undertaking. In the business of treasure hunting, one could never be too cautious. An eighteenth- or nineteenth-century manuscript from Lönsboda, Osby kommun, Sweden, for example, contains an extensive conjuration against "all trolls and mountain trolls and sorcerers...and earth wights and all kinds of evil spirits and poisonous ghosts" that might otherwise prevent one from extracting a buried treasure,[141] and another necromantic manuscript from Sweden includes defensive measures in case one should "see a

---

140 Rankine (2009), 85.
141 Nordiska Muséet 41.674, in Johnson (2019), 411–13.

ghost or revenant flare up from money".[142] Meanwhile, across the North Sea, Goodwin Wharton, in one of his many unsuccessful treasure-finding ventures, sought to employ a deceptively simple method of opening the earth by means of some magical hazel rods after Mary Parish's ghostly informer confirmed that a hillock near Hounslow contained a stash of riches guarded by the spirits of thirteen people who had buried it there.[143]

The association of ghosts and other spirits with buried treasure was paralleled in some regions by the belief that such treasures were categorically ensorcelled; Russian folklore gives us the adage *klad so slovom kladut*, "treasure is hidden with a [magic] word",[144] and an eighteenth-century Iberian treasure-hunting manual declares that "Moorish treasure is protected by

---

142 Nordiska Muséet 271.602, in Johnson (2019), 473. The wording here is not arbitrary, as a flare of fire has long been recognized in Germanic folklore as a sign of unquiet burial and, hence, likely hidden treasure; see for example chapter XVIII of the fourteenth-century *Grettis Saga*, where Grettir, upon witnessing just such an eruption, comments, "[I]f that were seen in our land, [it would be said] that the flame burned above hid treasure", to which Audun replies, "That fire I deem to be ruled over by one into whose matters it avails little to pry".

143 Clark (1984), 49–50.

144 Ryan (1999), 166.

magical art".[145] The previously-mentioned invocation from Sloane MS 3824 inquires as to whether a sought-after treasure "be kept by any Spirit or Spirits... Or by any artificial or magical Charms", and even offers an epistemological justification for the presumption that such custodians should be present, who are "as by the traditions of Man as rationally supposed, & so credibly reported unto posterity, & by good testimony thereof is verily believed of us, to be accustomary & usual for all such Treasures so hidden". [146] There again, persuading demons to procure these forbidden goods for oneself was not without its own caveats: as the *Raven* admonishes, "if the spirits wish to cause much trouble, or to make demands, then you must by no means allow them, and on your life do not comply, lest you come to great misfortune", and the Swedish necromantic handbook mentioned above enjoins that, should one employ its runes to "call forth all the spirits of hell, who watch over the hidden treasures", one must neither give nor promise them anything.[147]

Whether or not a trove was explicitly placed under magical or spiritual guard, treasure hunters had recourse to a variety of entities and technologies to assist them in locating and recovering it, not least

---

145 Biblioteca Nacional de Portugal, MSS. 155, n. 147. This text also ties such enchantments to the planetary rulership of the hour in which they are enacted, and the division of spirits presiding therein. In light of this, the table of planetary spirits in the *Raven* may play a more integral role within the manuscript's overall program than is superficially apparent.

146 Rankine (2009), 40.

147 Nordiska Muséet 271.602, in Johnson (2019), 467.

the beatified dead themselves. Along with God and his angels, the *Raven* invokes the Fourteen Holy Helpers, a group of saints that became popular in German-speaking lands in the fourteenth century, and one of them, St. Christopher, was widely regarded as a patron of those seeking buried riches. Although his historicity is questionable, and even the legendary accounts of his life make no clear association with material wealth, the manuals, prayer-books, and grimoires employed by eighteenth-century German treasure seekers did not fail to adduce their own apocrypha and *historiolae* legitimizing his role.[148] We might speculate that the ritual scheme of the *Raven* and its Faustian ilk appealed to an audience who perceived in the transgressive danger of negotiating with demons—perhaps tacitly hazarding their own immortal soul in the process—a degree of power or efficacy greater than that provided by the more sanctified magical prayers addressed to Christopher and other saints, yet, aside from the cast of characters they called upon, the prayers of treasure hunters frequently approached goetic conjurations or diabolic pacts in their formal structure, complete with apparitions, signed contracts, and a final banishing.[149] The rather equivocal regard in which these notionally divine paracletes were held was no anomalous innovation of a decadent post-Reformation folk theology; the hagiographies, *vitae*, and miracle stories of the Middle Ages reveal a relationship between saint and devotee that was widely construed as

---

148 Dillinger (2012), 85–6.
149 Dillinger (2012), 86–8.

transactional—complete with bribes, services in kind, and rebukes for non-fulfillment[150]—if not always so mechanically efficacious as the proverbial magic spell.

Conversely, the protagonist of a medieval ghost tale might face their ghastly tormentor with divine names and consecrated circles, conjurations to appear in a human form, and all of the usual rigmarole of exorcism, only to conclude by conscientiously asking after "the cause of his punishment and the remedy that belongs to it."[151] Indeed, the techniques of ghost laying attributed to English country parsons in local folk memory often bear a striking resemblance to the *nigrimantic* rites of demon conjuration ubiquitous in medieval grimoires. Cornish legendry tells of how, in the mid-seventeenth century, Parson Corker of St. Buryan once inscribed a warding circle against which the wrathful haunt of John Tregagle, villainous steward of Lanhydrock, Radnor, battered himself in the form of a black bull while Corker recited an exorcistic litany to bring him to heel.[152] Given the belligerent disposition evinced by this and other ghosts in need of ameliorating intervention by the living, the similarity in methods is perhaps unsurprising.

In early modern Poland, a spiritual accomplice of a distinctly different sort was ascribed to those suspected of coming by their prosperity via illicit supernatural means. The *latawiec* was an ambiguous being, variously conceived of as a household familiar,

---

150 Bartlett (2013), 106–12.
151 James (1924), 364–9.
152 Brown (1979), 29–30.

a demonic incubus, the soul of an unbaptized infant, or some indeterminate conflation of all of these, which stole the goods of others for the benefit of its master.[153] This "treasure-hauling imp" featured prominently in a number of seventeenth-century witch trials; Eva Lenartka of Warta accused her neighbors of keeping a *latawiec* that lived in their attic and brought them money, while Maria Karabinka's was said to fly from her chimney to bring her milk and grain.[154] Often described as a small bird with a tail of sparks,[155] this tame magpie was a storm-crow as well, its fugitive soul forever pursued by ill weather and lightning, crying out to be granted the Christian name—the very *Crystendome* that elsewhere we saw a cunning magus use to extort ghostly service—that would redeem it from consignment to the *limbus infantum*.[156] Sometimes known as *porońce* or *niechrzczeńce*—a name also applied to the mandragora

---

153 Ostling (2011), 225.

154 Ostling (2011), 199.

155 Ostling (2011), 205. Just slightly to the west, in eastern German lands, a very similar class of thieving familiar, sharing many of the *latawiec*'s complex characteristics albeit without any hint that it might be a wayward mortal soul, was much more frequently known to take the form of a dragon, rather than anything particularly avian (Dillinger, 2022). I will only note in passing here that the spirit Furfur, described in Johann Weyer's *Pseudomonarchia Daemonum* and its successor texts as a hart with a fiery tail, appears in a late fifteenth-century Italian manuscript in the likeness of a *crow* with a tail of flames (Biblioteca Medicea Laurenziana, MS plut. 89 sup. 38). In both presentations, the spirit bears some association with thunder and lightning as well.

156 Lehr (2014), 190; Ostling (2011), 203.

root, with its eerily fetal morphology and application as a prosperity talisman in Polish witchcraft[157]—these wayfaring children, like the other restless dead we have surveyed, sought to convey a last pending wish in the hope that someone might hear and fulfill it, setting them free.[158] The *latawiec*, unchristened yet innocent, was a liminal entity *par excellence*, partaking of the numinous powers of blessed and damned alike, in addition to that dangerous potency hanging like a miasma around the dead who fail to depart.

The belief that an unshriven soul might attract divine displeasure in the form of a tempest seems to have widely informed the mortuary lore and communal fears of early modern central Europe. A number of localities in seventeenth-century Bavaria were swept up in *Friedhof Aufruhre*, cemetery revolts, which entailed ejecting the corpses of suicides from burial grounds in order to forestall hailstorms provoked by God's wrath.[159] Likewise, in Austria, 1754, a hundred-strong mob prevented the burial of a woman who had taken her own life, fearing it would bring about thunderstorms.[160] In communities immediately dependent upon their own collective agricultural production, where bad weather could mean financial ruin or months of hunger, the wellbeing of the many superseded the sanctity of the individual, to say nothing of the norms of funerary propriety. The taboo of suicide, with all of

---

157 Ostling (2011), 201.

158 Lehr (2014), 201.

159 Lederer (2002), 37.

160 Luef (2012), 569–70.

its supernatural ramifications, was inflected by notions of communal responsibility and guilt, and the person who presumed to take their life in their own hands was also placing their body and soul beyond the pale of their society. That being said, spirits of the more generally ill-reputed dead seem to have tended to accrete similarly meteorological folkloric associations; in England's West Country, thunderstorms followed in the wake of particularly truculent ghosts, whether as a parting rebuke when exorcism sent them hurtling off to the Red Sea, an omen attending the ill-considered invocation of their name, or simply the atmospheric manifestation of their personality.[161]

As the *Raven* itself makes apparent, magical treasure-hunting manuscripts were not averse to recommending demonic assistants in addition to saintly intercessors and ghosts in one's quest to acquire a livelihood. Dillinger mentions—but refrains from identifying—one such text from the late seventeenth century, which features a demon introducing himself as Aziel, "a spirit of hidden treasures and goods which I hid as I liked and which I reveal and give to anyone I please and without me willing nothing is taken from me".[162] Allowing for the kind of transformations to which an indistinct phoneme can be subject (the voiced alveolar fricative /z/ slips quite easily into the voiceless /s/), to say nothing of the vagaries of copyists' handwriting, perhaps transplanting a proper name from its native Latin soil into a new German hothouse,

161 Brown (1979), 28–9, 62.
162 Dillinger (2012), 91.

this Aziel is no doubt identical—at least in spirit—with our own *Schatzmeister*, Aciel. Whether either one of them is the same as Arthur Gauntlet's "Asaciell the King of the dead Or the keeper of the bones of the dead",[163] the "Azazel Asiel" of "A true experiment for treasure hid, or for anything you would know" in another seventeenth-century manuscript,[164] or even Assasell, whom Humphrey Gilbert and John Davis recommended as the first spirit one should call when setting out on a conjuring career,[165] is left as an exercise for readers who would themselves delve after things deeply buried.

---

163 Rankine (2011), 235.

164 Newberry Library, MS Case 5017, 23, in Cummins and Legard (2020), 165.

165 British Library, MS Additional 36674, 47r–v, in Cummins and Legard (2020), 64–66.

VI.

𝔚𝔦𝔱𝔥 𝔖𝔞𝔟𝔩𝔢 𝔚𝔦𝔫𝔤𝔰

ON THE LETTER & SPIRIT(S) OF
DARMSTADT MANUSCRIPT 2543.

This present chapter forms a section-by-section walkthrough of the *Black Raven*, paying particular attention firstly to the Letter of the work—its material requirements, ritual actions, and the holy names, *daemons*, unclean spirits, and so-called 'barbarous words' mentioned—and secondly to the Spirit of the *Black Raven*: its advice *notae*, phrasings of the conjurations, and overall working ethos. We will use these components of the *Raven* to survey the range of similar (and dissimilar) arrangements in other Faustian grimoiric material. In presenting this survey we will consider the working technique, craft logics, and unfolding experiments of this text, furnishing the reader with a better understanding of the manners and methods workable to best operationalise this grimoire in their own work.

This chapter will also usefully frame some parts of the text's instruction which may be somewhat ambiguous or open to interpretation, and present both contents and contexts to help operators navigate such potential trip hazards in getting this *Raven* successfully off the ground and into flight. Perhaps the most significant issue concerns the lack of concrete instructions about the actual application and use of the seals, sigils, symbols, and even the exact nature of the series of so-called 'cryptograms' which the text vouchsafes.

To conduct this exploratory survey in a helpful manner, we will treat each section of the *Black Raven* in turn. By examining the grimoire's constituting parts, and how they relate to each other and its deeper context in devilish European grimoiric magic, we may explicate a great deal about the text's approach to folk nigromantic conjuration and exorcism. The manuscript is divided into seven sections: 'On the Blessing and Conjuration of the Circle', 'The First Prayer', 'The Second Prayer', the 'Summons and Conjuration' which includes both a general appeal to infernal superiors and 'the summoning of Aciel the master of treasures', the 'Summoning of a Haunt', a section on the names, sigils, and ministering spirits of the seven planetary archangels, and some concluding remarks to the 'good exorcist' intending to employ these magics. So let us look at said magics a little more closely.

On the Blessing and Conjuration of the Circle

The *Black Raven* opens with a brief rundown of initial instructions for preparing a circle of conjuration. Components of these magical approaches to circling are not unique to this manuscript, demonstrating grimoiric techniques comparable to both formal medieval conjuring manuals and early modern English nigromancies.

It becomes immediately apparent that the text does not include unique consecrations and exorcisms of *every* material component and tool of conjuration, although the method espoused frequently expects the item to be (already) 'consecrated'. While this may seem to produce "gaps" of needed material in this streamlined nigromancy, the *Black Raven* consistently repeats expectations to simply *do your usual* consecrations and so on; which is to say, the *Raven*'s approach already expects to be supported with your typical and supplementary grimoiric calls, consecrations, and conjurations.

Circling with Paper

Our first section presents a central requirement of 'parchment or virgin paper' i.e. paper not written upon and whitewashed clean as was once common. The paper is to be used to construct the circle of conjuration. The operator is expected to turn up at the *Raven*'s rite to 'bless and conjure' a parchment that has been previously 'prepared as usual'. The *Black Raven*'s manual of technical instruction begins by assuming the actual construction of this parchment circle has already been performed. This section actually even opens with '*when* the circle with all pertinent things is prepared as usual, from parchment or virgin paper which one must bless and conjure, *then* place two consecrated wax candles thereupon' etc. That the instructions for the operation continue with this '*then*' make clear this 'conjuration' of the circle-parchment should be done at the time of laying and consecrating the circle; that is, during the rite as well as a preparation of the paper beforehand.

If we are considering which 'usual' circle parchment preparations might be especially favoured for the *Black Raven*'s operations, we may examine other Faustian grimoires which frequently specify the use of paper circles. The most common form of this circle is one constructed of virgin paper, of a size of nine feet across, although there are other or different details across the corpus. *Magia Ordinis* allows the size of the circle to 'be chosen at will', and the *Embodiment of Unnatural Magic* likewise affords the circle can be 'as big as you want it'.[166] The *Almuchabola*'s must be constructed of 'goat's skin' but then clarifies or offers the alternative 'i.e. virgin paper'.[167] The *Magia Naturalis et Innaturalis* suggests either a circle of three rings 'made from good Dutch paper' which 'must be pasted onto canvas', or 'for the better, from virgin parchment'.[168] An experiment 'to summon three spirits to fetch gold' in the *Nigromantisches Kunst-Buch* requires a circle of virgin parchment, which it specifies is to be placed 'facing east in a hidden spot by the window.'[169]

It is also worth noting however that not all Faustian grimoires use paper circles. That of the *Herpentillis Salomonis* is drawn in chalk, 'more or less 2 to 3-feet

166 Nicolás Álvarez Ortiz & V. Velius (eds.), *A Compendium of Unnatural Black Magic* (Enodia Press, 2016), 50, 88.

167 *Compendium of Unnatural Black Magic*, 76.

168 Nicolás Álvarez Ortiz (ed.), *Doctor Johannes Faust's Magia Naturalis et Innaturalis: Threefold Harrowing of Hell, Last Testament and the Sigils of the Art* (Enodia Press, 2016), 10.

169 Benjamin Adamah (ed.), *An Early Grimoire of Demon Magic: Nigromantisches Kunst-Buch* (VAMzzz Publishing, 2024), 78.

long and wide'.[170] Perhaps the most elaborate Faustian circle is that of *Faust's Mightiest Sea-Spirit* which 'must be composed of a solid plate' of a three-cubit diameter, in which a triangle is 'placed'. This triangle must be composed of or bordered with 'three chains from a gallows, as well as nails from the breaking wheel, that sliced through the skin of a person broken at the wheel' which are welded together and soldered with copper between eleven and twelve o'clock on Good Friday, and hammered 'until it is big enough for the triangle' while invoking '[presumably Saint] Peter, [to] bind'.[171]

As has already been footnoted by my colleague Brian, one 'usual' grimoiric method of preparing a circle from parchment can be found in the *Liber Juratus* attributed to Honorius, in which a 'circle' is in fact seven strips of paper bearing names and seals of power laid out (and sometimes affixed with nails) in a loose heptagon. Given the importance of seven-part spiritual hierarchies and ritual actions in *Raven*—especially those of planetary magic and spirit-work—this seven-part circle encompassing the work would seem an especially apt ritual design.

We shall also return to practices of circling-with-parchment—whether "whole cloth" or piecemeal—and sigilated papers below when considering what to make of the *Raven*'s cryptograms and spirit-sigils at the end of this surveying chapter.

---

170 *Compendium of Unnatural Black Magic*, 101.

171 Nicolás Álvarez Ortiz (ed.), *Doctor Faust's Mightiest Sea-Spirit* (Enodia Press, 2016), 59.

Inks for Circles

Returning to the circle of the *Raven*, the ink with which it is to be drawn is again simply noted as being 'prepared as usual'. The circles themselves (and more often specifically the divine names, Scriptural versicles, and/or sacred characters) of other Faustian grimoires are most typically written in dove's blood—aside from the particularities of the inscribed names and characters in each grimoire's circle, there are also some variations to even this. *Embodiment of Unnatural Magic* specifies the inking blood must be from a white dove and must be written with a feather from a swan.[172] The names within the circle of *The Book of Mightiest Spirits* are specified to be written in 'male-dove-blood'.[173] The circle of the aforementioned operation for a trio of gold-fetching spirits is to be drawn in bat's blood.[174]

Some Faustian circle-inking directions are a little more complicated. In the triple-ringed circle of the *Magic Naturalis et Innaturalis* for instrance, the first ring's litany of names are written in blue ink; the Gospel of Saint John is written in the second ring in 'red sinople ink or better yet with white lamb or dove blood, both being male'; while the circle's third ring bears versicles (and, if there is still room, the names of Holy Patriarchs) in green ink.[175]

---

172 *Compendium of Unnatural Black Magic*, 50, 88.

173 *Compendium of Unnatural Black Magic*, 63.

174 *Nigromantisches Kunst-Buch*, 76.

175 *Magia Naturalis*, 10-11.

Candles

The *Black Raven*'s initial instructions then call for 'two consecrated candles' to be placed upon the circle. The exact consecrating words and actions for the candles are also not specified, suggesting an approach whereby one simply uses the consecratory techniques one would normally employ. This is not an uncommon condition in folk grimoires; of being required to perform *a* consecration but not necessarily any *specific* consecration. This reading is supported by the phrasing of the circling instructions more generally: 'when the circle with all pertinent things is prepared *as usual*'. The *Black Raven* does not purport to be a beginner's guide: it expects you to know your way around (at least preparing) a circle of conjuration and its attendant accoutrements.

Magia Naturalis has detailed instructions for constructing and consecrating candles. Firstly, they 'must be five in number, of which four go in all the four [cardinal] parts of the World and must be laid in the circle', once more highlighting the interrelationality of circle and candles. The fifth should be held by the operator 'so that [t]he[y] can see and read.'[176] Such an instruction is not only practical, but also shows that a Faustian conjuror was not necessarily expected to memorise all their calls, and furthermore that the act of reading from the book of calls seems to have utilized the power of the tome itself as a tool of sorcerous efficacy beyond being mere ritual script or reference material.

---

176 *Magia Naturalis*, 7.

These candles may be prepared in two manners. The first method simply requires that they should be 'burnt for their consecration with the wax-candles of an Altar [i.e. of a church]'. The second method involves making them from scratch out of tallow of a black young goat, 'a little brick oil', frankincense, myrrh (specified to be 'red'), a little ('virgin') sulfur, and white candle wax. These ingredients should be powdered (and presumably added to the wax) in the twelfth hour of Holy Night and formed around a wick woven by a seven-year-old child, before a consecration is read over them an hour after their creation.[177]

Ever the more explicitly and particular necromantic rite of the corpus, the Faustian *Sea-Spirit* operation requires all three of its operators to bear in their right hand 'a candle made from wax, which must have been burnt in the proximity of the death-bed of a corpse, and afterwards should be consecrated by a priest.'[178]

Suffumigating Circle & Candles
This section of the *Raven* also calls for the circle and/or candles to be suffumigated, although it does not specify any particular incense. We should be reminded that this does not seem an uncommon approach to conjuring either: the sixteenth-century English *Excellent Booke* for instance does not specify particular suffumigating ingredients, requiring merely 'great

---

177 *Magia Naturalis*, 7.
178 *Mightiest Sea-Spirit*, 59.

plenty of sweate powders, and perfumes'.[179] It seems the *Raven*'s nigromancy is of those approaches in which the specifics matter less than the affect: it must be good incense fit for its ritual purposes of course; but it does not need to be any particular incense beyond that.

Alternatively, the *Raven* may be reasonably read as requiring "the usual" conjuring incenses i.e. those commonly used in other works of this milieu of nigromancy. The Faustian corpus certainly offers more particular suffumigation formulary for operations of spirit conjuration: a mixture of aloes, myrrh, frankincense, black cumin and ivy (as given in *Magia Ordinis*); black poppy seed, hemlock, coriander, and an equal ratio of saffron and honey (as per the *Book of Mightiest Spirits*); a not-dissimilar blend of black poppy seeds, hemlock, saffron and celery, this time *all* in equal proportions (as in *Almuchabola*); white chicory, white elderberry, and lime tree flower (given in *Embodiment of Unnatural Magic*); or frankincense, liquid styrax, ship pitch, a piece of sulfur, aloeswood and half a piece of 'rhodium wood' (in *Herpentills Salamonis*).[180] Uncharacteristically, given its usually incredibly specific *materia* requirements, the operation of Doctor *Faust's Mightiest and Most Powerful Sea-Spirit* merely requires an incense of 'salt and [frank]incense'.[181]

While the *Magia Naturalis et Innaturalis* does not have a specific incensing component to its circle

---

179 Phil Legard & Alexander Cummins (eds.), *An Excellent Booke of the Arte of Magicke* (Scarlet Imprint, 2020), 89.

180 *Compendium of Unnatural Black Magic*, 52, 66, 80, 91, 100.

181 *Mightiest Sea-Spirit*, 59.

consecration, requiring merely the sprinkling of holy water, this grimoire does have far more extensive Faustian instruction for incense preparation and consecration necessary to proper 'disbandment' of the spirits: stipulating three sorts of incense with differing functions listed in chronological sequence over the course of such a rite.

1. The first incense is made of powdered frankincense, myrrh, mastic, and aloes (which should be purchased on a Sunday at twelve o'clock (that is, presumably at least, midday); this first recipe is employed 'at the first manifestation' of the spirit.
2. The second suffumigation is composed of cooper's pitch and sulfur. The exact function of this incense is not specified, but certainly falls between the incenses associated with the apparition of the spirit (the first) and a coercive compulsion of the spirit (the third); suggesting a use for charging or 'binding' the spirit to the task at hand once it has appeared.
3. The third recipe, 'a strong scourge of the spirits so that they can be coerced', is a powder of garlic, hellebore, and 'unused yellow sulfur'. It is also implied in the conjuration instructions for this incense's use that it may also expel the spirit, supporting its role in both forceful exorcism or perhaps even orderly dismissal.

All of these incenses are to be consecrated and stored in white paper. There also follow instructions in the *MN&I* for the brazier itself, which must be a new and unused iron or clay 'hollow-bowl' bearing unused charcoal, and must have the Consecration of the Brazier recited over it.[182]

Additionally, there is a deep root of planetary timing at the core of *Raven* which gives us an additional context for possible incense specifics. The standard planetary incenses—whether composed by individual planet as in the *Heptameron*, or as a consolidated sevenfold blend covering all of them at once—seem so widespread in treatises of highbrow theory and low-down working-books alike and so commonly used that the *Raven*'s lack of specificity may also indicate this sort of formulary could likewise constitute "doing the usual". In this case, we could be potentially observing an industry standard of sorts instead of, or indeed as well as, one's personal 'usual' *materia*, plant allies, and practices.

Conjuring the Circle

Once all these circle-pieces are assembled, blessed, and conjured, the conjuration of the circle itself includes a full declaration of intent: one is here to bless and conjure the circle, by the power of 'omnipotent threefold God' and a selection of popular divine names; to call spirits (specifying 'you evil spirits as well'); to impose some health and safety restrictions ('you shall absolutely not damage nor violate this circle, nor cause the least harm by accident or affliction to either me or my companions, neither in body not soul'); and ultimately to 'command all of you spirits'.

---

182 *Magia Naturalis*, 8-10.

When it comes to dealing with these minor and major devils and fallen angels, it is worth noting the conjuror will be later reminded in this text to be firm with the spirits summoned, some of whom may indeed try to cause trouble and misfortune for the operator.

A list of apparent names of spirits and/or words of power follows this conjuration. Our anonymous author of the *Raven* recommends us to 'divide... and demarcate each syllable distinctly, and thereby one can read everything back again.' These words are meant to be written as well as read aloud by the operator apparently, thereby once more foregrounding the necessity of one's own book of calls (if only a hand-scribed copy of the *Raven* itself) as a functional tool of the operation. It might even seem to suggest these words of power are to be written on the paper of the circle. We also find seven lines of cryptographic characters included after the previous advisory *nota* about proper grimoiric orthography for maximum sorcerous legibility. The Darmstadt manuscript then concludes its circle consecration with 'hereby I conjure this circle' and seals this stage of the work with an 'amen'.

With all these observances and actions rightly performed, we are told 'this circle is consecrated', and are instructed to proceed to a general opening prayer (appealing to God for blessing and protection), 'the following prayer' (for license to command spirits), and then the specific 'summoning of the spirit you wish to have'. These invocations and conjurations are all presented in useful chronological sequence following this first section on the circle in the manuscript. However, there is one final piece of procedural advice given between the completion of the circle's 'conjuration' (i.e. its consecration to ready use) and the following prayers: how to enter the circle.

Entering the Circle

We are told we should enter the circle praying for God's protection over 'our proceedings and our lives', and are specifically instructed to examine our companions 'as to whether they stand in grave sin'. This can be seen in light of grimoiric magic's usual understanding that conjuration is ineffectual or even dangerous if the operator is not properly and piously prepared. However rather than simply evidencing the necessity of a formal Confession as part of the usual old (i.e. Catholic) preparatory approach to this spirit-work, or even merely stating that the operator and their fellows must be of 'clean conscience' to work boldly and effectively (as in the 'Instructions of Cyprian' found in Arthur Gauntlet's working-book[183]), the *Raven*'s examination of our companions is framed a little differently. The examination seems an active endeavour by the operator to minister to and/or interrogate out the potentially guilty secrets of their fellows, specifically 'so that they can be answered by your apt reproaches, and you and your companions do not thereby come to misfortune'. It would seem we must deal—or at least make deals— with our own skeletons and shades within our circle if we wish to deal with those without it.

---

183 David Rankine (ed.), *The Grimoire of Arthur Gauntlet* (Avalonia, 2011), 39-40.

There are clear (post-)Reformation undertones to this assumption of priestly ministering by the conjuror. This *nota* also seems to show a sensibility of actively working to clear one's conscience through dialogue and the 'reproach' of one's summoning sodalities over the dogmatic letter of a hieratic observance of confession or set period of purifications. No taboo or fast or spiritual ablution can set your soul right *for* you, this approach seems to suggest, although these observances may well provide solid means, method, and opportunity to do so. Again, for the nigromancies of the *Black Raven*, doing *a sort of* confession seems more important than the specific rites of the confession. Outside of theological schismatics or technical ritual debate—and certainly without excusing a would-be grand magus trying to shame or otherwise lord it over their conjuring pals in the name of saving souls and/or ritual safety and efficacy—there is a glimmer of something practical in this advice. If one steps into circle to summon powerful spirits together with others, one should be sure those others can keep themselves together...

The First Prayer

This First Prayer is, as already introduced, a general opening invocation, imploring the 'beloved heavenly father' to grant 'luck, health, and blessing, in this our plan and work'. Its tone is thoroughly supplicatory, framing the conjuring party as 'we your children [who] beg humbly, with meek spirit' for God's blessing and protection in the present spirit-work at hand. It also asks the Almighty 'to send your holy angels to help us', proceeding to name-check all seven planetary archangels. We should thus be wary of considering the First Prayer mere pious preamble, for there are technical dimensions of the work—specifically its planetary timing—established and activated in this part of the summoning, as well as the prayerful appeal for the God of Hosts, Heaven and Earth to 'protect us from all evil.'

Following this First Prayer, the *Black Raven* actually combines a formal *letter-of* grimoiric conjuration approach with its shadier and more personal *spirit-of* ethos when it instructs 'hereupon pray a *devout* Our Father'. We pray with our hearts not just our words, the *Raven* reminds us.

This section ends with another six lines of Faustian cryptographic symbols, which rather leave us with more questions than answers about not only their identity or meaning but their function and utility.

The Second Prayer

The Second Prayer begins immediately following these somewhat mysterious six lines of glyphs. This incantation builds on the previous appeals for general blessings and protection from evil spirits to an entreaty for almighty God to 'give strength and power to the words of my mouth over the evil angels'. We have extended *protection from* into *power over* such unclean spirits. The tone of the Second Prayer thus moves from supplication (please God...) to empowerment (...make me mighty against evil spirits).

These spirits are also given a specific theological framing, being called 'evil angels who have been cast out of your holy Heaven into the Abyss'. Precedent as well as a cosmic order is thus affirmed—these spirits have been subject to God's commands (especially punishments) before after all. Moreover these 'devils' are still considered part of the whole ineffably divine order. Once more, the *Raven* is eminently practical, grounding this cosmic authority in tangible conjuration tactics: this Second appeal is made 'that I may compel and bind [these evil angels] to appear visibly in friendly human form before my circle, and to fully satisfy my words'. The appeal is empowered by choice 'holy names of your godly majesty' which are also carefully deployed to be explicitly intoned to denote the conjuror's own empowerment by them; that is, the conjuror calls those names which are then considered to be '*conferred upon me*, O you merciful God and beloved heavenly father'. A transfer of power is being conducted in this invocation of holy names.

The specification of binding devils to appear in 'friendly human form' seems grounded in a fundamental understanding that form stirs sympathies in functionality. If we read this intended friendliness as not only an affable appearance but moderating actual character and interaction, such conjuration to humane forms seems a (further) behavioural regulation of the spirit's manifestation. To compel a spirit to look more human seems a means to foster or force an overall more humane expression of the spirit, or at least the conjuror's encounter with it. This reading is further supported in a few *notae* contained in various goetic offices of the wider grimoiric corpus in which it is cautioned that certain spirits cannot be worked with safely and/or effectively without first assuming or even being compelled to assume human(e) forms.

The Summons and Conjuration

The third section of the *Raven* is formed of three interrelated entries. The first subsection adumbrates an infernal hierarchy of the 'many different sorts' of devils with which this grimoire deals. As with many such goetic adumbrations, its concision both streamlines ritual conjuration sequence, and also raises both conceptual issues and some lack of practical specifics. The second subsection collects the actual Summons conjuration, protocols, and sigils expected to license the operator with authority over infernal spirits by their senior ruling devils. The third and final subsection consists of a conjuration of Aciel, a spirit not previously mentioned in the *Black Raven*'s listed hierarchy.

A Mal-archy of Demonology

The *Black Raven*'s demonology rests on the infernal authority of Lucifer and Beelzebub, 'these being the infernal gods'. The Summons conjuration begins with conjuring by these senior 'foremost devils' over their 'followers'. It is notable, in the wider European nigromantic grimoiric corpus, dominated by triumvirate models of Hell's Chiefs—typically Lucifer, Belzebuth, and either Sat(h)an or Astaroth—that a third 'foremost' rank is not mentioned. Astaroth is however given as the first of the 7 'kings who stem from their infernal gods', along with two of the Four Kings of the cardinal directions, Egim and Paimon. The fourth king spirit, Mastroth, seems a copyist's clone—a grimoiric 'ghost' in Jake Stratton-Kent's terminology—and only further emphasises Astaroth as appearing to possess a further authority and agency beyond their express rank or role as Lucifer's 'principal' spirit. The fifth king, Asrica, looks to the present author like a version of Africa, a senior fairy of the Seven Sisters under Queen Mycob *aka* Micol, queen of the pygmies. The sixth, Storey, remains perhaps the most open to further study. The origins of the seventh, Cavocnz, also remains mysterious for now at least; although if we may permit ourselves to speculate it can perhaps be said to have a certain ring of Enochiana to it.[184] My point is that

---

184 Such a notion—of spirits drawn from the Angelical materials and experiments of Dr Dee appearing in wider spirit lists outside of explicitly "Enochian magic"—is not without some comparative historical precedent. Alan Thorogood has made a strong case for a number of the spirits listed in the appended 'Discourse' of the 1665 expanded edition of Reginald Scot's *Discovery of Witchcraft* having a basis in Meric Casaubon's *True and Faithful Relation* for instance: see Alan Thorogood, *Dr Rudd's Nine Hierarchies of Angels* (Teitan Press, 2013), x; citing Meric Casaubon, *A True and Faithful Relation of What passed for many Yeers Between Dr. John Dee (A Mathematician of Great Fame in Q. Eliz. And King James their Reignes) and Some Spirits* (London, 1659), 94-6. We also see recommendation of conjurational material concerning 'the good Angels of health' directly citing the Linea Sancti Spiritus of the so-called Enochian Tablet of Air in the medical cunning of William Williams' *Occult Physick or The three Principles in Nature Anatomized by a Philosophical opperation* (London, 1660), 125-126.

the identifiable spirits of the Faustian corpus already appear to be drawn from a wide range of sources, and we would do well to cast a wide net when looking for earlier appearances of these kings of hell. I encourage interested nigromancers to conduct their own research and experiment into these spirits.

Of course the seven kings 'have under themselves certain crowns and lordships' too, and particular attention is paid to seven princes who are 'subdued' under the kings, 'whose regency alternates'. These princes bear something of a resemblance—through the squinted mind's eye of reverse-engineering spelling variations and copyists' typos—to the names and exact sequence of the ruling aerial *daemons* of the days of the week listed by Honorius: the *Raven* giving Bareham for Barthan, daemon of the day of the Sun; Harthan, daemon of the day of the Moon, remaining faithfully unaltered; Gannax for Iammax, daemon of the day of Mars; Ambuma for Habaa, daemon of the day of Mercury; Juhbarmon most unfamiliarly for Formione, daemon of the day of Jupiter; Harabejes for Sarabocres (*aka* Sarabores), daemon of the day of Venus; and Mayton for Maymon (*aka* Hayton), daemon of the day of Saturn.[185] Such an alignment further fleshes out a layer of planetary virtue and affect in the *Raven*'s demonology—not to mention options for preferred timings of operations—that we shall see reinforced in

185 For further comparison of these seven kings across manuscripts, see Joseph H. Peterson (ed.), *The Sworn Book of Honorius: Liber Iuratus Honorii* (Ibis Press, 2016), 19-20; and Joseph H. Peterson (ed.), *Elucidation of Necromancy* (Ibis Press, 2021), 18.

both its necromancy and its core operating protocols.

It is a truism of this form of nigromantic spirit-work that spirits have under-spirits. The *Black Raven*'s demonology thus continues. The Princes have 'under them another 7 officers'. Many of these officers' names, in at least these forms, seem unfamiliar, although Ariabel/Aziabel is found in across Faustian texts (including *The Fourfold Harrowing of Hell* and various editions of the *Seventh Book of Moses*) as one of the 'seven serviceable great princes', with the *Seventh Book* listing them—alongside their fellow princes Aziel, Ariel, Marbuel, Mephistophilis, Barbuel, and Anituel—as 'a prince of the water and mountain spirits and their treasures', who is said to be 'amiable and wears a large pearl crown.'[186]

In other words, the infernal hierarchy of this *Black Raven* is a re-articulation of familiar senior devils and powerful spirits appearing in slightly different forms and ranks than their other instantiations across the goetic corpus. The ranks of 'kings', 'princes', and 'officers' evokes medieval handbooks' litanies and conjurations of angels and aerial spirits, yet the fundamental calling-structure of senior, deputy, and subordinate is also found in later nigromantic grimoires such as the *Grand Grimoire* and the *Grimorium Verum*.

Considering the variegated (not to mention occasionally badly-bootlegged) history of practical grimoiric demonologies and their rebellious spirits,

---

186 Joseph H. Peterson (ed.), *The Sixth and Seventh Books of Moses* (Ibis Press, 2008), 278; Migene González-Wippler (ed.), *The New Revised Sixth and Seventh Books of Moses* (Original Publications, 1991), 110.

we should recall this malarkey of infernal hierarchy is not itself un-traditional. Comparison can helpfully be drawn with the *dramatis personae* of the so-called *Bibliotechque Bleu* corpus, where a familiar rogues' gallery of devils is cast in a range of specific offices and positions of command across various iterations of the *Grand Grimoire* and its ilk.

A grimoire articulates practical power-structures between spirits not inviolate cosmology; as working grimoirists we need not *resolve* these strange articulations and variations across differing manuscripts so much as explore what actually works in terms of effective and sustainable conjuration. A few features—such as the two rather than three Chiefs and the peculiar mixture of spirits listed as the seven 'kings'—are unusual, but then again, folk nigromantic grimoires are usually unusual. Exploring these configurations of hierarchy and the offices of the spirits should furnish us both with an understanding of the uniquely-formulated qualities of *Raven* as well as presenting contexts for understanding the cast of devilish characters and conjurations which the Faustian corpus shares.

Moreover, this litany of shady spirit should remind us that although the *Black Raven* only explicitly instructs in one particular rite—the summoning of Aciel to help find and deliver treasure—this operation should rather more be taken as an exemplar or template to be employed for other spirits to be called, rather than the sole limits of the *Raven*'s wingspan. Once again, this grimoire seems to assume a certain competency—not to mention willingness and indeed aptitude to experiment—on the part of the nigromancer using it.

Conjuring by the Chiefs of Hell

The text of the first infernal Summons reads as an inter-cutting exchange of words of conjuration and the cryptogram signs. It begins with names of the 'foremost devils' and God, before interjecting two lines of glyphs. It then declares a further entreaty for God's protection; then offers four additional lines of glyphs. 'Beelzebub and Lucifer' are then formally addressed, which is followed by a line diagram of some kind, followed by a further call of *voces magicae* beginning 'Lucifer ✠ Rual ✠ Paymon et omnes spiritus', before settling into the vernacular of the conjuration. This conjuration contains a number of pertinent phrasings— the two devil chiefs are conjured 'once more' in an implicit appeal to conjurational precedents, as well as by a 'living, holy, and undivided God': emphasising the indivisible one God as Lord of Hosts over the many divided legions of fallen spirits. This singular answer to a multitude of devilish questions also conveniently explains the 'spirit N' insertion of this more standard conjuration boilerplate. This conjuration is explicitly designed to be a part of work with other spirits beyond Aciel.

The last part of this Summons & Conjuration section is the conjuration of what we might term the actual spirit we expect to appear, answer, and work. Whereas our previous Prayers and even the Summons seem the standard conjurations for all operations, this final call requires the specifics of name. The *Raven* provides a labeled seal for Lucifer and Beelzebub and for Aciel, which bear markings remarkably similar to the recurring Faustian cryptograms. We are even told 'each spirit has their own sign': which at the very least affords the possibility of using the sigils given for these spirits when they are listed in other catalogues. Even with the seals of Lucifer, Beelzebub and Aciel, we know *who* they are for but are still no closer to concrete instructions on how we may helpfully employ them however, beyond an inferred directive of *doing our usual* with them. Further study of Faustian techniques for working spirit-sigils will be analysed near the end of this chapter's survey.

A Lord of Treasures

This final modular stage of the *Raven*'s central or exemplary operation is to call 'a lord over all hidden treasures of the earth' who is conjured to 'fetch out this hidden treasure, which has been displaced from human hands, from the same place where it lies'. We should again note that Aciel is regarded in the singular—*a* lord and master of treasures (i.e. amongst many other spirit-lords of treasure)—and moreover that such treasure hunting magic also frequently (at least implicitly) assumes the spirit is called not simply to *locate* buried gold or whathaveyou but to *disenchant* various sorceries that magically displace the treasure 'from human hands' to make it even possible to not only find but exhume and acquire.

Further presenting the possibility of working the *Black Raven* for conjuring spirits beyond those it categorically mentions, we should note that Aciel is not a spirit explicitly named in the *Black Raven*'s earlier hierarchical breakdown; highlighting that the *Raven*'s listed hierarchy is not exclusively limited to work solely with the kings, princes, and officers officially name-checked, but may form a nigromantic backbone and navigable structure by which the conjuror may flesh out operations with spirits of the wider corpus. In this, the *Raven* appears to implicitly state what other grimoires make plain: there exist spirits beyond those listed, and these others may also be worked with according to these protocols and techniques.

Aciel is certainly a significant spirit in the Faustian corpus. In the *Magia Naturalis et Innaturalis* Aciel is hailed as the fourth Grand Prince of Hell, the senior Solary spirit of the seven Prince-Electors of the Devil, alongside Bludon—which is (also) an alias of Lucifer himself—as well as Lunary Barbuel/Marbuel, Mercurial Ariel, Saturnine Barbiel, Jupiterian Mephistophiel, Martial Apadiel ('*seu* Gamael'), and Venusian Anael.[187] Such a senior spirit is afforded many conjurations or 'citations' in *Magia Natural et Innaturalis* concerning the delivery of treasure and how to demand it in increasingly coercive manners.[188] It is also written that 'his regent is called Raphael', a relationship evoked later in the *Black Raven*'s streamlined license to depart.[189]

Aciel is also hailed as one of one of the seven Wise Spirits—amongst Mephistophiel, Barbiel, Marbuel, Ariel, Apadiel, and Camniel. Significantly, the one Wise Spirit here who is not also a Grand Prince or Prince-Elector is the Count Palatine Camniel who is described as a close servant of Aciel and is said to be

187 *Magia Naturalis*, 24.
188 See for instance *Magia Naturalis*, 33-54.
189 *Magia Naturalis*, 33.

placed as a guardian of treasures. The Grand Prince Aciel also holds command over the seven Counts: Radiel, Dirachiel, Paradiel, Amodiel, Ischabadiel, Casadiel, and Jazariel according to the *Magia Naturalis et Innaturalis*.[190] This last spirit is especially important in matters of dealing with the haunting dead, for the spirit Jazariel, who appears 'as a wise serpent', is said to be the 'chief of all tribal-spirits'—the English term Álvarez Ortiz appears to render for *Stammgeist*–who 'brings them forth from the air'. Given Jazariel is also called 'the wisest and cleverest spirit', it is therefore unsurprising that their name is invoked in the *Black Raven*'s opening litany.[191] Once more, we should note that even the *Raven*'s barbarous words of conjuration have an illuminating context within the milieu from which they were formulated.

Nor should the multiple appearances and job-titles of Aciel within the Faustian grimoires be considered unusual for this spirit. The spirit Aciel themselves has been identified as likely synonymous with a spirit known widely and variously across the wider European corpus of nigromantic texts as Aquiel, Acquiot, Foras, Parcas, Annobath, and Surgat; each alias complete with its own sigil and frequently a slightly different set of emphases of this spirit's characteristic purviews and powers. In other words, this is a spirit that does not seem to mind turning up in different manners wearing

---

190 *Magia Naturalis*, 16-17, 71, 66, 67.

191 *Magia Naturalis*, 117. It is Álvarez Ortiz's opinion that 'the "tribal spirits" that appear in the *Magia* are ghosts that guard treasures.' *Magia Naturalis*, xxv.

different hats.[192] The manifold forms and functions of this spirit demonstrate there are indeed consistent craft logics and even familiar *dramatis personae* across the Faustian tomes. Furthermore it highlights that these spirits are not limited to appearing and functioning within this particular grimoiric operating system. Spirits are not owned by the books that hold the variously formulated secrets of their conjuration.

The question of the breadth of applicability of the *Black Raven*'s conjurations—of just which and how many spirits will answer to these calls—becomes worthy of consideration. It seems the *Raven* demonstrates, at least implicitly, a capacity to summon more spirits than simply Aciel or the others it mentions in the charting of its senior devils. It also seems pertinent to note that in the wider Faustian corpus, a range of prayers, citations, and even a circle of Aciel are used for a variety of spirits serving under them, from the seven Counts to Camniel the senior Count Palatine.[193]

---

192 For more on Aciel's wider appearances across the grimoiric papertrail, see Jake Stratton-Kent, *Pandemonium: A Discordant Concordance of Diverse Spirit Catalogues* (Hadean Press, 2016), 35, 165-171; see also Jake Stratton-Kent, *A Prince Among Spirits* (Hadean Press, 2016).

193 In the *Magia*'s chapter on 'Deals with the Seven Counts', it is instructed: 'the Grand Prince Aciel holds command over these and all shall be called with his main citation and circle.' *Magia Naturalis*, 67. Aciel's 'answer' concerning his offices and role also states 'my Count Palatine Camniel, who is my servant, serves humans. He receives Strength and power from me, and in my name, in order to serve with the same power as I would; but without me, he can do nothing, therefore I must always be with him.' *Magia Naturalis*, 33-34.

As we shall shortly assess, the inclusion of the Summoning of the Haunt in *Black Raven* immediately after this present Conjuration offers options to both conjure a treasure-hunting spirit and lay a haunting spirit, which we might frame more broadly as both binding a spirit to perform a task and loosening a spirit to be 'put at their liberty'. We may be usefully reminded of archaic Greek *goetic* conceptions of spirit-work as matters of such binding and loosing.

At the culmination of these Summons & Conjuration instructions within the present manuscript, the spirit is finally summoned and conjured to speak 'in a friendly form in my familiar language' to the conjuror, once more emphasizing the affability of the encounter as well as highlighting the insistence that exchange is understandable by at least the conjuror if not the spirit as well. We may be reminded of wider examples of conjurations for magical knowledge specifying that the spirit who brings good books of magic also delivers 'the understanding' of such potent texts too.[194] This seems a framing coverage against demons fulfilling the letter but not spirit of the request—such as specifying they deliver in a language comprehended by the operator – but also once more demonstrates that conjuration can also be conducted to learn and develop our sorcery *from* conjured spirits as well as simply doing magic with them.

---

194 The *Excellent Booke* for instance presents protocols for dealing with a situation in which Oriens may 'hath brought you A booke in the stone to yor sighte... yf you can not reade it... to showe me the readinge and understanding of yt'. *Excellent Booke*, 91.

The conjuration winds up with repeated injunctions of protection, that the spirit carry out its charge and deliver 'without any terror or fright, hail, deceit, or blinding, nor harm to the circle nor my and my companions' bodies and souls'; concluding with a thrice-called injunction to 'come!' in both vernacular and then Latin. Aciel is commanded by the incantation of 'Nisza ✠ Hagal ✠ Ligkama Raphael', again apparently underscoring the importance of planetary as well as archangelic authorities in the *Raven*. Wider reading of Aciel's offices in the Faustian demonological corpus previously mentioned (especially that his 'regent' is Raphael) demonstrates such angelical namedropping was not random, but an operative citation attesting an understanding of a working relationship between planetary angels and devils—in this case, Solary Aciel and (occasionally Solary[195]) Raphael—in these Faustian modes of nigromancy.

A brace of seals and a symbol are then given, and the tone of the final conjuration once again shifts to addressing the spirit on the one hand as 'you acclaimed angel', yet on the other emphasizing 'you who are cast out from the throne of God, you who shall be weighted down with a thousand souls, you who have been cast

---

195 While typically considered the archangel of Mercury in (more modern) grimoiric angelologies, Raphael is the primary angel of the Sun in older texts such as *Liber Iuratus* (see *Sworn Book of Honorius*, 203, 320). This Solary association is also present in many of the manuscripts containing material pertinent to the *Elucidarium* family of grimoires, such as Clm 849, Halle 14 B 36, Leipzig Cod. Mag 40, and others. See Peterson, *Elucidation of Necromancy*, 268.

into the torment of Hell, and have been forsworn from the womb'. It would seem this final section of the conjuration acts as a malediction of sorts to be intoned if the spirit does not answer to the previous triplicate calls to come. Both divine and infernal authorities are invoked as the operator identifies and empowers themselves declaring 'I too have come to that place by the Devil's power, and appoint to this place from beneath their heavy burden Adonai, the high prince Gabriel, the prince Ninive... and their emissaries, and you, holy Niniverus'. Aside from the (possibly pseudo-) medieval specifics of this bevy of divine names, once again the indivisible Almighty empowers of the conjuror against the manifold unraveling legions of the diabolic: the cunning exorcist declares these words and seats of power to assert that they themselves 'have been joined with you, and so the Devil shall not divide them, and so the Devil shall not divide you'. The call is sealed with three crosses.

Summoning of a Haunt

The incantation of this 'Summoning' opens immediately with a direct address to the 'haunting spirit', then defines and locates this target by both specifying it by its habitat as well as offering a range of alternative environs—'who dwells in this house (or barn)'—further highlighting that this specification might be subject to substitution or modification as context requires. A parallel to this haunted house is also somewhat evoked in the appeals of this conjuration to be effective 'by the prayer of the whole Church' (lit. *Geistenheit*), evoking the House of the

Lord and the community of the congregation as well as a clear overarching ecclesiastical authority.

Invoking God's power frames the encounter as a classic work of grimoiric conjuration: the operator directly appeals to 'the sacrosanct Trinity [which] shall threaten and compel' the spirit to 'appear to me visibly', to assume (its previous) human form, and that the spirit will, rather typically, 'have neither peace nor rest until you fulfill my will.' One fascinating departure from the usual conjuration of unclean spirits (such as the devils of the goetic grimoires) should be noted of the form one expects the spirit to take. For while we might mistake this for yet another imperative to conjure to human appearance for ease and affability of exchange, the specific framing and exact phrasing is clear: we expect the spirit to appear 'in *your true* human form'. Let there be no question about what sort haunting spirit this working is intended to deal with and 'put at liberty': it is clearly the ghost of a deceased human.

14 Holy Helpers

The Summoning of the haunt conjures 'by the 14 Holy Helpers' as well as by the 'strength and power' of God and the angels in Heaven. This group of sainted figures, also known as the *Nothelfer*, the "Need-Helpers" or 'Helpers-(Of-Those)-In-Need', rose to prominence in the fourteenth century and consist of Agathius, Christopher, Giles, Denis, Blaise, Erasmus (*aka* Elmo), Vitus, Pantaleon, Cyriacus, Eustace, George, and the 'three holy maids', Margaret, Barbara, and Catherine (of Alexandria). Many of these helping saints were considered to aid against specific ailments—prayers and petitions were made to St Blaise specifically for healing and protection of the throat, for instance.

This hagiographic appeal in our conjuration of the haunting spirit provides a variety of saintly patrons for the 'good exorcist' working the *Black Raven*, offering a range of helpful auxiliary observations such as litanies, prayers, and chaplets, as well as a ritual calendar of feast days to mark and potentially employ in ritual purifications and other forms of conjuring preparation and work. The Fourteen Holy Helpers were for a time from the fifteenth century celebrated on a collective feast day of 8th August in some parts of Europe, although this no longer appears to be on the official Vatican books.

These fourteen saints seem to have been initially gathered together and invoked as a collective by the pressures and petitions arising from the Black Death which ravaged across Europe from 1346 to 1349. It is supposed that the unique patronages and intercessions of this convocation of saints offered an especially apt set of protections against the maladies of plague which included the blackening of the tongue, throat pain, severe headaches, boils across the abdomen, and fevers:

> Among the saints invoked since the earliest times of the Church as special patrons in certain diseases were: St. Christopher and St. Giles against the plague, St. Dionysius against headache, St. Blase against ills of the throat, St. Catherine against those of the tongue, St. Erasmus against those of the abdomen, St. Barbara against fever, St. Vitus

against epilepsy. St. Pantaleon was the patron of physicians, St. Cyriacus was had recourse to in temptations, especially in those at the hour of death; St. Achatius was invoked in death agony; Sts. Christopher, Barbara, and Catherine were appealed to for protection against a sudden and unprovided death; the aid of St. Giles was implored for making a good confession; St. Eustachius was patron in all kinds of difficulties, and, because peculiar circumstances separated him for a time from his family, he was invoked also in family troubles. Domestic animals, too, being attacked by the plague, Sts. George, Erasmus, Pantaleon, and Vitus were invoked for their protection.[196]

The cultus of the Holy Helpers was further strengthened by a series of visions in Bavaria in the mid-fifteenth-century, culminating in the building of a chapel dedicated to the Blessed Virgin and these fourteen saints which was completed in 1448 at the site of the visitations 'when, in the course of time, several extraordinary favours were granted to people who prayed at the place of the apparition'.[197]

Significantly for reading the *Black Raven*, and especially (the candles of) its circling rites, it should be noted that the Helpers appeared not only as a child to a

---

196 Fr. Bonaventure Hammer, *The Fourteen Holy Helpers* (Benzinger Brothers, 1909), 2-3.

197 Hammer, *Fourteen Holy Helpers*, 5.

young shepherd, Herman Leicht, in September 1445—
and then again as a group of fourteen children nearly
a year later in June 1446—but by a striking vision: 'The
following Sunday, after [Leicht] had driven his flock
to pasture, it seemed to him that he saw *two lighted
candles* descending from the sky where he had seen
the apparition. A woman who was passing at the time
declared that she also saw them.'[198]

That the *Raven* calls for two lighted candles within
the circle of conjuration should not be taken as entirely
or exclusively owing to this vision—after all, debates
about the correct number of altar candles raged
throughout the buildup and fallout of the Reformation
and it is important to note that various Protestant
denominations from Lutheran to Anglican favour no
more than two candles—it is however a further context
for understanding the Christian folk nigromancy of
the practices and worldview to which this manuscript
attests.

Meeting, Greeting & Departing

Another instance of a battery of triplicate prayers
follows the initial summoning conjuration, directing
the operator to say '3 Our Fathers'. Following this
we are given the 'Greeting of the Spirit' which offers
further understanding of the purpose and methodology
of this conjuration. Upon the spirit appearing—
presumably in the time between the Summoning and
the completion of these Pater Nosters—we are to greet
the spirit as 'welcome'; despite such a haunt also being

---

198 Hammer, *Fourteen Holy Helpers*, 5. Emphasis added.

identified as 'defiant' and 'willful', we are nevertheless to at least attempt 'to accommodate' them. We are to encourage the spirit to speak in order to tell us 'by what means he may be set free'; specifically 'what time and hour he would be put at liberty.' The grimoiric timing of planetary days and hours is, as we shall see, the underlying subject of the very next section of the *Black Raven*, and this seems the specific intention here: to locate the *planetary* time, hourly *spirits*, and indeed archangelic influences best suited to assisting this soul relinquishing any hold in the mortal coil. Having discerned this timing, we are instructed to 'send him on his way' with a peaceful dismissal. The psychopompic role of helping a "stuck" ghost pass over is clear.

Compulsions and abjurations seem mostly employed to insist the haunting spirit show up. Once the haunting one does manifest to us, our exchange is rather more persuasive than commanding. We are to begin by asking the ghost '*if* he would be released from his circumstances', and then 'by what means'. The very fact we determine how (and specifically when) to act by asking the spirit what *they* want shows a different power dynamic from typical demonic operations. We are after all only threatening the spirit ultimately with the good time of either Heaven or at least peaceful rest until Judgment.

The dismissal itself, also instructed to be repeated thrice, is one of sending the spirit off peacefully. Another slight manipulation of conjuration is worked here: for the spirit is allowed or directed to 'go there in the peace of the Lord', which is specified as 'the peace of God which is higher than all human reason and all ghostly capacity'. There is a confirmation both of the difference of operator and haunt and a reconciliation of both under the power of the Almighty. Moreover, this dismissal licensing the spirit's departure is literally worked by this peace, a force more powerful than either party, which also acts 'between me and you as a firewall and a separation', specifying, 'such that... you can do me no harm'. The spirit can only depart if it acknowledges its inability to hurt the operator, for—as the dismissal ends asserting—'the most holy Trinity stand by' the conjuror.

This operation dealing with the haunting spirit can and should be understood in its manuscript context as a modular operation in the treasure-hunting conjuror's kit for certain eventualities. Seeking treasure magically can involve disenchanting the magics hiding it and dealing with the (haunting) spirits guarding or otherwise tied to it and/or the land in which it is hidden. There are many kinds of unfinished business. We should also understand the operation in its own ghost-light, as it evidences these more fundamental folk conjuration approaches to spirits-that-haunt which offer the enterprising nigromancer vital contexts and operative techniques for dealing with such hauntings.

Planetary Spiritwork

A sevenfold list of the planetary archangels is then introduced and delivered, presenting the usual planetary glyphs for Michael, Gabriel, Samael, Raphael, Sachiel, Anael, and Casiel. Their sequence follows the days of the week, rather than a Ptolemaic or 'Chaldean' ordering of the planets by distance or qabalistic arrangement; again, likely highlighting an influence of the *Heptameron* and its related texts and practices.

This litany of 'holy [arch]angels' is followed by a further sevenfold list of the senior Olympian spirits, referred to as 'the 7 Kings', along with their '7 Officers'. These Olympians 'Kings' seem an exceptionally popular set of spirits found throughout Germanic grimoiric texts. Research published by Benjamin Adamah in their German Occult Manuscripts in Translation series has highlighted a range of texts from the sixteenth to nineteenth centuries detailing a variety of approaches to these planetary spirits: from the sevenfold lists of 'highest', 'middle', and 'lower' forms of magical results which diligent work with these seven spirits may yield the operator who properly marks its threefold occult philosophical considerations and the forty-nine 'Aphorisms' familiarly iterated in many versions of the *Arbatel*, to the singular conjuration of Aratron in *Dr Faust's Coercion of Hell* by an inscribed forked hazel wand, circle, and a unique sigil of Prince Araton 'of the Air' written in raven's blood placed under one's right foot, in order to be granted a familiar spirit.[199]

Within these Faustian Olympian works are a range of other magical resources and operations, such as the names of God in seventy-two languages to 'write and call in four letters' and a talismanic tablet, plate, or

---

199 Benjamin Adamah (ed.), *5 Early Grimoires of the Olympic Spirits* (VAMzzz Publishing, 2024), 24-54, 113-114.

parchment with a range of folk magical applications in the *Arbatel de Magia Veturum*.[200] Crucially, there are also many developments of characters specifically relating to the seven Olympians themselves. Various editions of the *Magia Naturalis* present configurations of the characters and pentacles of the seven Olympian spirits (and for use in work with their under-spirits), including a grand seal 'arrangement' for all seven 'Olympic or planetary angels or governors', individual planetary sigils for the '7 Planetary Princes', and seven double-sided Olympian pentacles which embellish the familiar glyphs.[201] An experiment for *A True and Brief Description of the Mercury Rod* includes planetary pairs of fourteen geomantic characters alongside the "standard" Olympian sigils to be marked on the seven metals smelted to form this 'electrum' rod.[202] Notably, the *Black Raven* demonstrates this Faustian manner of presenting alternative or additional sigil designs and arrangements in listing its own idiosyncratic glyphs for either (or perhaps both?) the Olympian 'kings' and/or their 'officers', which bear a striking resemblance to its cryptographic material; including riffed adaptations of astrological glyphs, such as a sideways zodiacal glyph

---

200 *5 Early Grimoires of the Olympic Spirits*, 97-101.

201 For the 'arrangement and seat of the throne angels, and the seat of the so called Olympic or planetary angels or governors', see *Magia Naturalis*, 157 and plate 118. For '*sigilla* or *pentacula* of their 7 Planetary Princes counted according to their order from [Sun] or Och', see *Magia Naturalis*, 157, and plates 119-125. Alternative double-sided designs are evidenced in *5 Early Grimoires of the Olympic Spirits*, 123-129.

202 *5 Early Grimoires of the Olympic Spirits*, 133-137.

of Cancer for Bethor, and what appears to be a form of Aquarius' waves for Ophiel.

While the *Black Raven*'s 'Kings' are the familiar cast of *Arbatel*'s Olympians–with Phul Germanised as Pfuel–their 'Officers' bear names not otherwise found within this Olympian strain of planetary magic. Derdiel, Asfariel and Miseriel at least bear the obvious angelic-looking suffixes; Jachiel is listed as the spirit of Leo's thirtieth degree in the Ars Paulina of the *Lesser Key of Solomon*. Seraphiel is an Enochic fallen angel, a chief of the Seraphim; similarly, Sateriel may be a rendering of Sathariel, another Watcher of the Enochic fallen angels. Salomiel is eerily reminiscent of not only Solomon, also commonly rendered 'Salomon', but perhaps of Salome. These named 'officers' of the *Raven* present a further Faustian development of Olympian spiritwork; one which it should be noted appears well within the bounds of established *Arbatel* protocols, which frequently afford that these senior spirits both grant subordinate spirits and may reveal further particular names and characters to the operator who successfully conjures them. Moreover, the inclusion of these 'officers' seems to therefore demonstrate not only the usual offices of the Olympians to give familiars, but the likely potential of the Raven-scribe to have actually worked with them sufficiently–or to have had access to the practitioners who have, or at least their texts evidencing such work–to receive and relay such names and sigils of these under-spirits.

A further list of twelve names is then imparted, presenting somewhat jumbled forms of the names of the hours from the *Elucidarium* tradition which informed the *Heptameron*: while the name of the first hour, Maduth, seems new, Janor is faithfully unchanged from the *Heptameron*'s rendering of Ianor; Salla, the original fourth hour has been rendered Sullu, and placed at the *Raven*'s third hour; the *Heptameron*'s third hour Nusnia has been replaced with Nusma and numbered the *Raven*'s fourth hour; Sadedali has become Sedethi; Thamur, Thumen; Ourer (mis)copied to Curen; Thamic to Taris; Neron, Neroa; Jayon, Jaxon; Abai, Abur; and Natalon, Nulbuon.[203] I am somewhat loathe to dismiss these entirely as misread gibberish—although many seem to have originated in such copyist errors—on the grounds that spirits of grimoiric magic have plenty of historical precedent for presenting slightly different or even secret operative names, such as the systems from which these *Heptameron* adaptations are derived. Until further research and experimentation has ruled it out, we should not be so quick to correct what may be the *Raven*'s "nicknames" for these hours and/or their spirits. Then again, if "doing your conjurational usual" involves a more standardized set of hour-names, the *Raven* seems to offer some of its characteristic flexibility in this regard.

A short gloss for the accompanying sigils explains their specific function for the conjuror: 'they are to be called on each day of the week'. We therefore have lists of the names (and in some cases, sigils) of the archangel, king, officer, and hour for each day of planetary working. We may be once more reminded of the three-step

---

203 See Peterson, *Elucidation of Necromancy*, 189, 228-231, 266.

hierarchy of navigating infernal conjurations, as seen earlier in the 'Summoning & Conjuration'. However the addition of the *Heptameron*'s names of the hours also demonstrates the *Black Raven*'s fundamental operating protocols owe something to the broader *Elucidarium* family of grimoiric systems. Crucially, in the discovery of a timing to be derived from questioning a summoned haunting spirit immediately preceding this section—in which the conjuror insists the spirit name 'what time and hour' to work to liberate the haunt—we have a definitively folk necromantic application of these hours and the planetary spirits called in them.

Parting Advice

The final section of the *Raven* concludes with a parting summary of its black art to the reader as a prospective operator. As is customary of many spirit lists and catalogues, we are reminded these spirits may 'fulfill all that you will'; yet, as is also somewhat customary, the would-be operator is reminded of the dangers of such work. A tight rein must be held over spirits who 'wish to cause much trouble, or to make demands'. This seems especially pertinent to note in light of the *Raven*'s approach to haunting spirits: attempting to accommodate does not mean being a doormat. Crucially, this tight rein is characterized both in summary and throughout the text as one of not *allowing* such troublesome conduct, and of not *complying* with such demands. Despite the parting advice warning of 'great misfortune' to the life of the unwary conjuror, there is more of a firmness of action and sense of consequences from a lack of firmness than an outright antagonism of hostility emphasised in this model of effective spirit-work. Beyond the usual sort of conjurational threats of (further) damnation, no specific techniques of actually torturing spirits are included in the *Raven*. The battle-dance between conjuror and spirit seems rather more one of wits and wills than talismanic weapons or warfare.

Such is the text that the anonymous author of the *Black Raven* commends as itself 'an extraordinary treasure', and encourages us to 'hold in esteem and high honour' as the means to 'bind and compel and conjure the spirits'. We are reminded that this is done that the spirits 'shall serve you perfectly', and indeed '*must* bring to you everything' you ask of them. Once more, a cosmological necessity of the properly-executed work's efficacy seems emphasised.

The Cryptograms

On the heels of such claims of efficacy, it seems pertinent we turn to the matter of the lines of glyphs found throughout the *Black Raven*, which exist without explanation or apparent instructions for their utility. Are they (partly) additional characters for the circle, and if so why are they separated in the manuscript? Are they to be written to be displayed or affixed to the breast of the operator for divine license, conjurational authority, and/or spiritual protection as they incant the First Prayer, as with plate of the *De Nigromancia*, or the Solomonic Pentacle of the *Heptameron* and so many other grimoires? If so, should they also be worn or carried by any assisting fellows? Most speculatively, are these glyphs perhaps even to be "spelled out" in the air while praying our pious Pater Noster like more elaborate forms of the signs of the crosses found in many grimoiric liturgies and conjurations?

Consulted in private correspondence, it is the opinion of expert on grimoiric seals and sigils Mihai Vârtejaru that these cryptograms are just that: enciphered text. Such cryptographic techniques were (and still are) used mnemonically as well as cryptographically—to help the conjuror memorise the ritual scripts of their calls, conjurations, and citations, as much as hide them from the eyes of others. We certainly see examples of such "conjuror's shorthand" in grimoires such as the *Clavis Inferni*.

The cryptograms certainly seem most often sandwiched between the conjurations themselves: indeed, that the glyphs of the *Raven*'s first cryptogram are found between the *nota* concerning phonetic pronunciation and the ending of the consecratory conjuration of the circle would especially seem to support this reading of them as a ritual speech-mnemonic. Moreover, the *Raven*'s cryptograms are often located in the midst of conjurational speech acts, and offer further evidence (along with the instructions concerning best copying the lettering of its conjurations for maximum legibility) that this grimoire was actually worked and not simply a spooky-looking folk necromantic fake fabricated to amuse or deceive.

Such ciphers are often highly personalized for the individual operator, and in the absence of a key by which to unlock these texts, further study of other manuscripts by the same scribing magician must be sought and analysed. Each glyph might indicate as little as a syllable, although they are more commonly used to refer to a whole spirit name or 'barbarous word', and might even encompass as much as a whole part of speech commonly employed in conjuration, such as boilerplate appeals to Trinity and so on.

Requiring a much broader and deeper analysis of more of the Raven-scribe's works and *notae*, such a cryptographic endeavour to definitely decode these Faustian puzzleboxes falls rather outside of the purview of this modest study of the *Black Raven* and the folk necromancy of Germanic texts and tradtions, but should perhaps be taken less as a stumbling block to working the *Raven* so much as a further mystery by which we might more deeply engage with it. We the present commentators of this edition of the *Raven* leave them to you to explore and decode.

In the meantime, the cryptograms may provide us not only opportunities for respectful consideration of this grimoire's historical use but an actual conjurational advantage by including these glyphs in our own handcopied working-books of the *Raven*, despite not currently fully understanding their original meaning. After all, magicians use all sorts of other 'barbarous words' and glyphs whose literal meanings are now lost to time in our magics. If the cryptograms do provide something more than notes-to-self of the original conjuror, and actually magically affect the spirits called, presumably the spirits themselves will remember their meaning. As such, it seems fruitful to suggest these glyphs might be engaged with, even knowing they are likely cryptographic and not yet deciphered, as additional characters to perhaps even show spirits or adorn ritual spaces and tools, to mark at least acknowledgement of the albeit-still-private secrets of the magician(s) who came before us and composed this work. Such experimental engagements would seem an appropriately folk necromantic answer to a folk necromantic question after all.

Ultimately only practical sorcerous *experimenta* can answer if these questions, concerns, and lines of practical inquiry can spur and develop (more) efficacious conjuration. Once again, we would do well to remember the *Raven* is not a "complete" handbook of conjuration, by which every single detail, protocol, tool, technique, and procedure is laid out for the conjuror; nor is it trying to be. It may fall to the cunning and ingenuity of modern readers and practitioners to engage with these shrouded facets themselves to help their *Raven* operations to further spread their sable wings.

The Sigils of the Spirits

Unlike the encrypted glyphs of the cryptograms, we can be sure that the labelled markings of the spirits mentioned in the *Black Raven* are indeed those spirit's sigils: and as such the issue of exactly how to use them is somewhat easier to address and thus present a range of options by which they may be employed. To establish our analysis, we must first draw attention to two other related but distinct forms of conjurational characters: Solomonic seals and name-papers.

Lamen & Conjuring-Seals

While many Faustian grimoires provide sigils for the unclean spirits one may wish to conjure, usually presented alongside their offices and purviews explaining what benefits or services these entities may provide, it is admittedly less common to find specific directions about the actual use or deployment of these spirits' characters. In contrast, the specific uses of various one-size-fits-all lamens, seals, sigils, pentagons, 'mortagons' (or 'Mathagons') typically associated with the figure of Solomon—by which the operator conjures and adjures potentially *any* spirit—seem far more commonly explicated.[204]

It is important to note we do find examples of techniques for employing protective and authoritative lamen and conjuring-seals adapted to the workings of spirit-sigils. Some English goetic manuals which include sigils of their catalogued demons instruct that one should 'make & wear [the sigil of the spirit] *as a Lamin* in time of acction &c.'[205] As we shall examine below, the attachment of characters to a wand or rod is another apparent adaptation of conjuring-seal protocols in using spirit-sigils common to Faustian grimoires. But such a(n albeit porous) distinction between 'Solomonic' lamen and spirit-sigils is important to understand in order to most fruitfully experiment and adapt further uses.

---

204 See for instance, the 'Instructions for Creating and Using the [Solomonic] Figures', *Nigromantisches Kunst-Buch*, 103.

205 See, for instance, Sloane MS 3825, 110v and *passim*. Emphasis added. See Joseph H. Peterson (ed.), *The Lesser Key of Solomon* (Weiser, 2001), 7-39.

It should also be noted that the chief distinction between a conjuring-seal for all spirits and a spirit-sigil for a particular entity is one of generality/specificity rather than an inherently "friendlier" approach of the latter. While this may not be the limited extent of the latter, both are employed for compelling spirits. As we shall examine in more depth below, the *Magia Naturalis et Innaturalis* refers to both 'coersive characters' and 'coercive sigils' for particular spirits such as Aciel, Annael, *et al.*[206]

Name-Papers

A further distinction is also worth noting between spirit's names and their sigils. The instructed and explicit uses of name-papers seems more frequent than those of spirit-sigils. While these are not the same thing, survey of such spirit catalogues' directives and protocols offers broader conjuring ethos, approaches, and craft-logics relevant to the use of spirit-sigils, as well as some options for the adaptive conjuror.

In the experiment from the *Nigromantisches Kunst-Buch* for conjuring three gold-fetching devils, the names of Astaroth, Berith, and Belzebub must be written on (the same piece of) virgin parchment and placed in the left shoe; the conjuror is also directed to wear a pair of shoes 'made from the skin of a coal-black dog'.[207] Papers marked with the characters of the spirit are also often used in actions of compulsion for dealing with recalcitrant conjurees: 'if they do not appear, then

---

206 *Magia Naturalis*, 53, 55, 62.

207 *Nigromantisches Kunst-Buch*, 76.

write their names on virgin parchment, and make a fire of sulfur and pitch', over which the conjuror holds the marked paper, threatens and eventually performs maledictions, and may even throw the paper in the fire.[208] Such techniques are far from unique to the Faustian corpus.

While these protocols for name-papers do not include or mention sigils for these spirits, the fundamental techniques might well be adapted: reminding us the placement and manipulation of papers bearing the markings of spirits is not limited to drawing them inside circles or triangles.

Coercive Writings

Significantly for the question of how to source sigils for spirits mentioned without their seals, the *Magia Naturalis et Innaturalis* actually details how one may use a type of name-paper to actually receive a full spirit-sigil directly from the very spirit themselves. Particularly pertinent to Raven-work, this sigil is for none other than Aciel:

> If you want to have the Coercing character of Aciel, then go and buy 1 *Granum Sasabaramimy* [i.e. a gram of saffron]... and 1 Piece of Dragon blood [resin], from these make an ink and write with it the following words on a paper:
>
>> Jesus fincit Aciel pars Christe Komtla Aciel O Adonay Domis Aciel, quas Agla Dortonoy o Aciel Jehova et quas Filii pors Aciel.

---

208 *Nigromantisches Kunst-Buch*, 92.

When you have finished writing, lay it far from the circle and cite him as the above written citation reads; and as soon as he comes he will immediately see the writing with great consternation, but do no fear. Through these words he will leave you his coercing sigil, and through the sigil you will learn all arts. You may obtain in the world whatever you want, in construction, in languages, digging treasures. Then when I take the coercive writing and lay it in the house, I should not touch it, I can know how much and what it is, and I can coerce him through that, so that he must bring me the money to my room. Also I can know through the coercing sigil who talks good or bad about me, or I can know, what this or the other does, or intends.

Given Aciel's sigil is one of the few actually already disclosed in the *Black Raven,* we may not need to perform this specific operation for Aciel. However the underlying technique certainly suggests a means by which conjurors may receive sigils for the other spirits mentioned in the *Black Raven:* as 'in *summa* it is the greatest secret in the nigromance, and when you want to know a secret, cite then the spirit and write a letter about the secret, and these words in it; thus he will bring you a written answer to you[r] requests.'[209] Not only does this highlight that the ink and words of this 'coercing writing' are not exclusively tied to receiving

---

209 *Magia Naturalis*, 53-54.

Aciel's sigil and may be employed for discovering other spirits' sigils, it also foregrounds the importance of Faustian sigil-reception, mark-making, and indeed conjurational epistemology. Nigromantic questions require nigromantic solutions.

Rods & Sigils

By far the most common Faustian use of the actual sigils of the spirits is in conjunction with a rod of some kind. In these cases, a staff or wand is employed to manipulate the sigil-papers of its spirits: often employing the long rods to hang or flourish these demonic characters outside the borders of the circle, as well as sometimes to strike the inked sigil to punish a spirit that does not adequately fulfill the operator's desires in an agreeable or timely manner.[210]

The specifics of this sigil-dangling rod vary somewhat. *Magia Ordinis* calls for a three-span ebony rod written on in black lamb's blood; the *Albuchamola* asks for a hazel stick written on with dove's blood; *The Book of the Mightiest Spirits* instructs its hazel stick be engraved in specifically white dove's blood; the *Embodiment of the Unnatural Magic* requests a four-spans-long rod cut from a white-husked tree-trunk that is marked in weasel blood.[211]

---

210 *The Book of Mightiest Spirits* for instance recommends 'if the Master has a business which the spirits resist to accomplish, he should take his rod, and hit with it the sigils, and puts those close to the fire or coals' to enforce "cooperation". *Compendium of Unnatural Black Magic*, 67.

211 See *Compendium of Unnatural Black Magic*, 50-52, 64, 77, 89.

Such techniques of attaching characters to an implement to reach across a circled barrier are worthy of contrast and comparison to the use of the scepter and plate of *De Nigromancia*. In this case, the characters employed are not the signatures of the spirit, but the fourfold name of God, Tetragrammaton (supported by the additional use of planetary characters), which empower the operator and compel the spirits. In other words, *De Nigromancia*'s characters are conjuring-seals like the Solomonic varieties mentioned above; they are not sigils of the summoned spirits. However, we can well frame the Faustian technique—of "fishing for spirits" with their characters on the end of an extended wand— as itself an adaptation of conjuring-seal techniques for using spirit-sigils.

Once again, while the *Raven* does not detail or explicitly require any such rod-work in its procedures, given its general ethos of working with circle and so on to be 'prepared as usual' it seems reasonable to posit such actions and additional tools evidenced in other Faustian works could form part of the conjuror's typical operating procedures ported into Raven-work. It is also worth consideration more generally that the *Raven* has little to no explicit spirit-compulsion techniques; which could be taken to imply either a less antagonistic approach to spiritwork, or simply the assumption that the competent conjuror already has other means at their disposal to employ should such need arise.

Circles & Characters

We may also usefully compare the *Raven*'s spirit-sigils (and indeed its circle-paper) to the procedures of the sixteenth-century English 'Book of the Science of Nigromancy' contained in MS Sloane 3853 (referred to as the *Book of the Dannel*) which uses parchments bearing the characters of spirits alongside a more familiar traced circle. In its initial (indeed, initiatory) procedure for 'Binding the Spirits Enclosed by Asmoday', the *Science* instructs: 'And then vpon the forthe daye after you shalt cause all the delves and sprytes of all the chapitores to obeye on to the[e], make a serkyll upon the earthe in a Desertt or a solytarye place, then write all the carectares of all the chapitores abovt the serkyll, in paper.'[212] Moreover, following the pact of this initial Binding of all the 'chapters' or working-groups, the deployment of an 'Applied Conjuration'—an operation of a particular working-group of the *Science*'s spirits—is effectuated by following the directions to 'chose what chapter you wyl worke in, and licence all the rest to depart, and make you a serkyll with a spere whose staff ys wyllow. And about the serkyll make the karecteres of the same chapyter which ye wyll worke in, and sence the serkyll with frankynsence.'[213] While the circling spear of the *Science of Nigromancy* may seem somewhat unusual, it is also found in the wider Faustian corpus. A 'special experiment on how to bring a good spirit into a glass' in the *Nigromantisches Kunst-Buch* identically details a circle created 'with a spear, the handle of which is willow', while also affording that the circle might be

---

212 Janneke Stam, 'A Book Called the Dannel: An Edition and Study of Sixteenth century Necromancy', Unpublished MA thesis (Radboud University, 2017), 220r.

213 Stam, 'Dannel', 235r.

efficaciously traced 'with other instruments'.[214]

Pertinently to our present considerations of what to actually do with spirits' sigil-papers, the *Science* presents the conjuror with an option to in fact do without an inscribed circle at all when working 'Applied Conjurations': 'if you wyllnot make a serkyll, leve the karecteres of the same chapteres [of spirits] with you and ye shall obtayne all your porpose in lyke maner *as yf ye had a serkyll* by the grase of god.'[215] In other words, the cast circle of the *Science*'s 'Applied Conjurations' seems optional, while the papers bearing the spirits' characters are not; and indeed may be carried on our person to act as a sort of portable circle of conjuration itself as well as sorts of "petition papers" to the working spirits conjured.

Sigil Materia

However we might employ and experiment with spirit-sigils, the wider Faustian corpus is far more explicit in presenting a variety of traditional options for their creation and marking: prescribing bat's blood on black goat's skin, 'coal-black raven blood on black virgin paper', and even 'black raven's blood on the skin of a black goat'.[216] Our *Black Raven* comes indeed from a thoroughly and occasionally literal blackly magical tradition of Faustian nigromancy.

Other manuscripts offer actual ink recipes for drawing figures, such as the *Nigromantisches Kunst-*

---

214 *Nigromantishcs Kunst-Buch*, 61.

215 Stam, 'Dannel', 235r. Emphasis added.

216 *Compendium of Unnatural Black Magic*, 51, 65, 79.

Buch's formula of lampblack made from the smoke of frankincense, myrrh, and spikenard combined with gum before dissolving. This ink is to be used to write a particular figure 'and also the incantation on virgin parchment of lamb or calfskin'.[217]

On the other hand, wider European nigromancies also employ simpler inks. The *Excellent Booke* for instance merely requires certain coloured inks to be 'had', with no requirement for creating them from scratch or with particular *materia*.[218]

These contextual comparisons of different approaches to sigilising inks are presented as experimental options for the enterprising nigromancer to further explore the magic of the *Black Raven*. To reiterate a consistent theme, the use of one's most familiar inks of the art would seem perfectly in line with the *Raven*'s ethos of doing one's conjurational usual. All colours will after all agree in the dark.

Conclusions

The *Black Raven* is a grimoire that does things in sevens and in threes; indeed it calls specifically on the strength and power of the Trinity. This Trinitarian power is called to compel spirits to human(e) forms by the planetary influences and timings of both the archangels and the Olympian ruling spirits and their ministers. It is not a grimoire with a lot of specific ingredients or even tools, rather operating through threefold appeals

---

217 *Nigromantishcs Kunst-Buch*, 102.
218 *Excellent Booke*, 89.

to ruling spirits, deputies, and subordinate officers via streamlined conjurations navigating a mosaic of hierarchy and sevenfold offices drawn and developed from the wider grimoiric corpus.

Having combed the feathers of the *Raven* we may quite reasonably come to ask: how *practical* is this grimoire? Questions of practicality in conjuration, and around grimoiric manuscripts especially, tend to focus on matters of completeness and workability. To deal with the first matter more immediately: the *Black Raven* is certainly no one-stop-shop. Its infrequent instructions to do one's 'usual' consecrations, observances, and ritual actions alone mark it as a text for conjurors with previous experience if not possession of (or at least access to) other books of calls from which to draw supporting as well as foundational material and techniques: for circle, candles, and protocols of spirit-sigil use at the very least.

The Raven-scribe's advice about phonetically spelling out *voces magicae* for best legibility and pronunciation by flickering midnight candles—not to mention the aforesaid examples of *doing the usual*—does seem to suggest a text that was actually used however. It certainly offers few formal restrictions on being brought into an extant conjuration practice. It is itself a text frankensteined in significant part, as we have seen, from potent sections of the *Heptameron* and *Arbatel*, as well as foregrounding less well-known spirits and demonstrating some unique characteristics, formats, and proceedings. Such are typical features of a working grimoire.

It should be admitted a few technical details *might* require some testing to get the most out of this grimoire. The names of hours and spirits taken from older conjuring sources seem riddled with fluxing mutations—but then so are most grimoires from an age prior to the standardization of spelling. I leave it to the investigative conjuror to join us in discovering which of these "re-articulated" names work as operative alternatives and which are merely inert miscopies.

More broadly, the lack of instructions or explanation on the various cryptographic lines of glyphs might suggest to ceremonialists and completionists a text less than actually workable as originally intended. But the history of early modern practicable working-books evidenced conjurors working far more through piecemeal assemblage and experiment than by any formalist sense of perfected reconstructionism or unassailably complete knowlededge. The aim of cunning operators was—and can remain—to actually work with spirits; not simply quibble and henpeck with our contemporaries or lodge-members or forum-frenemies about corrections or lacunae in the source material.

Our necromancer forebears seemed to have little compulsion about picking over the bones of old (and sometimes less-than-fully-understood) grimoiric works for solid components with life still in them for their own conjuration work. A raven is a carrion bird after all. Experimenting with (and developing) sections or techniques from the *Raven* might itself even be considered a form of engaging with the unliving spirit of its nigromantic tradition.

A few thus-far-inexplicable pieces does not necessarily a broken grimoire make. A conjuror's extant patrons and tutelary spirits may well be conjured to help provide stabilizing strategies for working a patchy grimoiric text and an incomplete understanding of how to get it up and running, as may careful examination and strategisation by divination. The manuscript record of working grimoiric conjurations evidences a rich if somewhat furtive tradition of editing and re-articulating templates as well as occasional substitutions of specifics as the techniques, formats, and protocols are adapted towards various ends. As always, such re-articulations rely ultimately on the fluency and eloquence of the conjuror's cunning.

𝔅ibliography

MANUSCRIPTS

Biblioteca Medicea Laurenziana, MS plut. 89 sup. 38.
Biblioteca Nacional de Portugal, MSS. 155, n. 147.
Universitätsbibliothek Leipzig, Cod. mag. 97.
Universitäts- und Landesbibliothek Darmstadt, Hs. 2543.
Weimar, Herzogin Anna Amalia Bibliothek, F 4348.
Weimar, Herzogin Anna Amalia Bibliothek, F 8476.
Weimar, Herzogin Anna Amalia Bibliothek, Hs. Q 455.
Weimar, Herzogin Anna Amalia Bibliothek, Hs. Q 455[b].

PRIMARY SOURCES

Adamah, Benjamin (2024). *5 Early Grimoires of the Olympic Spirits*. VAMzzz Publishing.
Adamah, Benjamin (2024). *6 Early Grimoires of Magical Lore*. VAMzzz Publishing.
Adamah, Benjamin (2024). *An Early Grimoire of Demon Magic: Nigromantisches Kunst-Buch*. VAMzzz Publishing.
Agrippa, H. Cornelius (2021 [1533]). *Three Books of Occult Philosophy*. Eric Purdue, trans. Inner Traditions.
Álvarez Ortiz, Nicolás & V. Velius (2016). *A Compendium of Unnatural Black Magic*. Enodia Press.

Álvarez Ortiz, Nicolás (2016). *Doctor Johannes Faust's Magia Naturalis et Innaturalis: Threefold Harrowing of Hell, Last Testament and the Sigils of the Art.* Enodia Press.

Álvarez Ortiz, Nicolás(2016). *Doctor Johannes Faust's Mightiest Sea-Spirit.* Enodia Press.

Anonymous (1680). *A Most strange and dreadful apparition of several spirits & visions at several times seen and spoken to, on the 14, 15, and 16th of this instant July, 1680, at the house of Mr. John Thomas, Junior, next door to the Sign of the Crown, at Cow Cross, in the parish of St. Sepulchres, London ... : with many more circumstances not here related, but will be certainly justified for truths, by the (credible) spectators.* Early English Books Online Text Creation Partnership, 2011, https://quod.lib.umich.edu/e/eebo2/A51476.0001.001/1:2?rgn=div1;view=fulltext, accessed 6 November 2021.

Anonymous (1691). *A true relation of the dreadful ghost appearing to one John Dyer in VVinchester Yard near St. Mary Ovres in Southwarke; taken to be the spirit of his late wife Jane Dyer, who departed this life some time since, with an account of the affrightful shapes, and its pursuing him from place to place. Likewise is added another account of the penitent murtherer, Robert Congden, who was executed in Brook-street, near Ratclif-Cross, and afterwards hung up in chains between Mile-End and Bow.* Early English Books Online Text Creation Partnership, 2011, https://quod.lib.umich.edu/e/eebo2/A63680.0001.001/1:2?rgn=div1;view=fulltext, accessed 6 November 2021.

Anonymous (1680?). *Great news from Middle-Row*

in Holbourn, or, A true relation of a dreadful ghost which appeared in the shape of one Mrs. Adkins to several persons, but especially to a maid-servant at the Adam and Eve, all in a flame of fire on Tuesday-night last, being the 16th of this instant March, 1679. Early English Books Online Text Creation Partnership, 2011, https://quod.lib.umich.edu/e/eebo2/A41924.0001.001?rgn=main;view=fulltext, accessed 6 November 2021.

Anonymous. "Grettir's Saga". William Morris & Eirikr Magnusson (trans.). *Icelandic Saga Database*, Sveinbjorn Thordarson (ed.), http://www.sagadb.org/grettis_saga.en, accessed 16 December 2022.

Anonymous (1743). *Nigromantisches Kunst-Buch, handelnd von der Glücks-Ruthe, dem Ring und der Krone Salomonis, den Fürsten-Geheimnissen, den dienstbaren Krystall- und Schatz-Geistern und andern wunderbaren Arcanen : Nach einer Handschrift aus der Bibliothek eines Fürst-Abtes im vorigen Jahrhundert wortgetreu und mit allen Abbildungen veröffentlicht : Der wahrhaftige englische Schlüssel Salomonis ... / Nach dem wahren Original verdeutscht und mit Abbildungen.* Peter Hammer's Erben.

Anonymous (1675). *The Rest-less Ghost: or, Wonderful News from Northamptonshire, and Southwark.*

Anonymous. "The Saga of Thrond of Gate". F. York Powell (trans.). *Icelandic Saga Database*, Sveinbjorn Thordarson (ed.), http://www.sagadb.org/faereyinga_saga.en, accessed 16 December 2022.

Cummins, Alexander, and Phil Legard (eds.) (2020). *An Excellent Booke of the Arte of Magicke.* Scarlet Imprint.

Casaubon, Meric (1659). *A True and Faithful Relation of What passed for many Yeers Between Dr. John Dee (A Mathematician of Great Fame in Q. Eliz. And King James their Reignes) and Some Spirits.* London.

Duling, D. C. (ed., trans.) (1983). Testament of Solomon. In James H. Charlesworth (ed.), *The Old Testament Pseudepigrapha, Volume I: Apocalyptic Literature and Testaments,* 935–987. Doubleday & Company, Inc.

González-Wippler, Migene (ed.) (1991), *The New Revised Sixth and Seventh Books of Moses.* Original Publications,

Haile, H. G. (1965). *The History of Doctor Johann Faustus.* University of Illinois Press.

Harms, Daniel, James R. Clark, and Joseph H. Peterson (eds.) (2015). *The Book of Oberon: A Sourcebook of Elizabethan Magic.* Llewellyn Publications.

Horst, Georg Conrad (ed.) (1821). *Zauber-Bibliothek, oder von Zauberei, Theurgie und Mantik, Zauberern, Hexen, und Hexenprocessen, Dämonen, Gespenstern, und Geistererscheinungen [...] Zweiter Theil.* Florian Kupferberg.

Heydon, John (1662). *The Harmony of the World: Being a Discourse wherein the Phaenomena of Nature are Consonantly Salved and Adapted to Inferiour Intellects.*

Hubert, Jürgen (2022). *Lurkers at the Threshold: 100 Ghost Tales from German Folklore.* JürgenWerks.

James, M. R. (ed.) (1924 [1922]). Twelve Medieval Ghost Stories. A. J. Grant, trans. *Yorkshire Archaeological Journal* 27: 363–379.

Johnson, Thomas K. (ed.) (2019). *Svartkonstböcker: A Compendium of the Swedish Black Art Book Tradition.* Revelore.

Lichtheim, Miriam (ed.) (1980). *Ancient Egyptian Literature, Volume III: The Late Period.* University of California Press.

Marathakis, Ioannis (2011). *The Magical Treatise of Solomon, or Hygromanteia.* Golden Hoard Press.

Peterson, Joseph H. (ed.) (2001) *The Lesser Key of Solomon.* Weiser.

Peterson, Joseph H. (ed.) (2008). *The Sixth and Seventh Books of Moses.* Ibis Press.

Peterson, Joseph H. (ed.) (2009). *Arbatel: Concerning the Magic of the Ancients.* Ibis Press.

Peterson, Joseph H. (ed.) (2016) *The Sworn Book of Honorius: Liber Iuratus Honorii.* Ibis Press.

Peterson, Joseph H. (ed.) (2021). *Elucidation of Necromancy.* Ibis Press.

Rankine, David (ed.) (2009). *The Book of Treasure Spirits.* Avalonia.

Rankine, David (ed.) (2011). *The Grimoire of Arthur Gauntlet.* Avalonia.

Scheible, Johann (ed.) (1846). *Das Kloster. Weltlich und geistlich.–Zweiter Band.* Expedition des Klosters.

Scheible, Johann (ed.) (1849). *Doktor Johannes Faust's Magia Naturalis et Innaturalis: oder, Dreifacher Höllenzwang, Letztes Testament und Siegelkunst [...] in fünf Abtheilungen.* J. Scheible.

Scot, Reginald (1886 [1584, 1665]). *The Discoverie of Witchcraft.* Brinsley Nicholson, ed.

Shakespeare, William. *Hamlet.* Barbara Mowat, Paul Werstine, Michael Poston, and Rebecca Niles (eds.), Folger Shakespeare Library. https://www.folger.edu/explore/shakespeares-works/hamlet/read/1/1/, accessed on 8 July 2023.

Stam, Janneke (2016). *A Book Called the Dannel: An Edition and Study of Sixteenth century Necromancy*. MA Thesis: Radboud University.

Thorogood, Alan (2013). *Dr Rudd's Nine Hierarchies of Angels,* Teitan Press.

Williams, William (1660). *Occult Physick or The three Principles in Nature Anatomized by a Philosophical opperation*, London.

SECONDARY LITERATURE

Baron, Frank (2013). Faustus of the Sixteenth Century: His Life, Legend, and Myth. In J. M. van der Laan and Andrew Weeks (eds.), *The Faustian Century*, 43–64. Camden House.

Bartlett, Robert (2013). *Why Can the Dead Do Such Great Things? Saints and Worshippers from the Martyrs to the Reformation*. Princeton University Press.

Bischoff, Wilhelm F. (1823). *Die Geisterbeschwörer im neunzehnten Jahrhundert oder die Folgen des Glaubens an Magie aus Untersuchungs-Acten dargestellt vom Großherzoglich Sächs.* Johann Karl Gottfried Wagner.

Brown, Theo (1979). *The Fate of the Dead: A Study in Folk Eschatology in the West Country after the Reformation*. Folklore Society.

Clark, J. Kent (1984). *Goodwin Wharton*. Oxford University Press.

Csapodi, Csaba (1969). The History of the Bibliotheca Corviniana. In Csaba Csapodi, Klara Csapodi-Gardonyi, and Tibor Szanto (eds.), *Bibliotheca Corviniana* 11–34. Corvina Press.

Davies, Owen (2009). *Grimoires: A History of Magic Books*. Oxford University Press.

Davies, Owen (2023). Print Grimoires and the Democratization of Learned Magic in the Later Early Modern Period. *Entangled religions* 14(3). https://er.ceres.rub.de/index.php/ER/article/view/10440/9928, accessed 16 April 2023.

Dillinger, Johannes (2012). *Magical Treasure Hunting in Europe and North America: A History*. Palgrave Macmillan.

Dillinger, Johannes (2022). The Dragon as a Household Spirit: Witchcraft and Economics in Early Modern and Modern Sources. *Magic, Ritual, and Witchcraft* 17(2): 212–240.

Dillinger, Johannes, and Petra Feld (2002). Treasure-Hunting: A Magical Motif in Law, Folklore, and Mentality, Württemberg, 1606–1770. *German History* 20(2): 161–184.

Doering-Manteuffel, Sabine and Stephan Bachter (2004). The Dissemination of Magical Knowledge in Enlightenment Germany. In Owen Davies and Willem de Blécourt (eds.), *Beyond the Witch Trials: Witchcraft and Magic in Enlightenment Europe*, 187–206. Manchester University Press.

Ebert, Friedrich Adolf (1830). *Allgemeines Bibliographisches Lexikon–Zweiter Band*. F. A. Brockhaus.

Edwards, Kathryn A. (2012). The History of Ghosts in Early Modern Europe: Recent Research and Future Trajectories. *History Compass* 10(4): 353–366.

Ferber, Sarah (2002). Reformed or Recycled? Possession and Exorcism in the Sacramental Life of Early Modern France. In Kathryn A. Edwards (ed), *Werewolves, Witches, and Wandering Spirits: Traditional Belief & Folklore in Early Modern Europe*, 55–75. Truman State University Press.

Hammer, Bonaventure (1909). *The Fourteen Holy Helpers*. Benzinger Brothers.

Harms, Daniel (2019). "Thou Art Keeper of Man and Woman's Bones" – Rituals of Necromancy in Early Modern England. *Thanatos* 8(1): 62–90.

Heeren, Arnold H. L. (1793). *Ideen über die Politik, den Verkehr und den Handel der vornehmsten Völker der alten Welt*. Vandenhoek und Ruprecht.

Henning, Hans, and D. L. Paisey (1978). An Addition to the Faust Literature: An Unknown 'Harrowing of Hell' in the British Library, London. *The British Library Journal* 4: 1–7.

Honan, Park (2005). *Christopher Marlowe: Poet & Spy*. Oxford University Press.

Kirk, Robert (1893 [1691]). *The Secret Commonwealth of Elves, Fauns, & Fairies*. Andrew Lang, ed. David Nutt.

Klaassen, Frank, and Sharon Hubbs Wright (2021). *The Magic of Rogues: Necromancers in Early Tudor England*. Pennsylvania State University Press.

Koslofsky, Craig M. (2000). *The Reformation of the Dead: Death and Ritual in Early Modern Germany, 1450–1700*. Palgrave Macmillan.

Lehr, Urszula (2014). Cultural Aspects of the Spiritual Legacy of Podhale Highlanders. *Ethnologia Polona* 35: 181–210.

Lederer, David (2002). Living with the Dead: Ghosts in Early Modern Bavaria. In Kathryn A. Edwards (ed), *Werewolves, Witches, and Wandering Spirits: Traditional Belief & Folklore in Early Modern Europe*, 25–53. Truman State University Press.

Luef, Evelyne (2012). Punishment Post Mortem – The Crime of Suicide in Early Modern Austria and Sweden. In Albrecht Classen and Connie Scarborough (eds), *Crime and Punishment in the Middle Ages and Early Modern Age: Mental-Historical Investigations of Basic Human Problems and Social Responses*, 555–576. De Gruyter.

Maly, Tomáš (2015). Early Modern Purgatory: Reformation Debates and Post-Tridentine Change. *Archiv für Reformationsgeschichte - Archive for Reformation History* 106(1): 242–272.

Marshall, Peter (2002). *Beliefs and the Dead in Reformation England*. Oxford University Press.

McKeever, Amanda Jane (2010). *The Ghost in Early Modern Protestant Culture: Shifting Perceptions of the Afterlife, 1450–1700*. PhD thesis, University of Sussex.

Moreira, Isabel (2010). *Heaven's Purge: Purgatory in Late Antiquity*. Oxford University Press.

O'Lynn, Aidan Anthony (2018). *Ghosts of War and Spirits of Place: Spectral Belief in Early Modern England and Protestant Germany*. PhD dissertation, University of Bristol.

Ostling, Michael (2011). *Between the Devil and the Host: Imagining Witchcraft in Early Modern Poland*. Oxford University Press.

Ryan, W. F. (1999). *The Bathhouse at Midnight: An Historical Survey of Magic and Divination in Russia*. Pennsylvania State University Press.

Scribner, Robert W. (2001). Lyndal Roper (ed), *Religion and Culture in Germany (1400-1800)*. Brill.

Scurlock, Jo Ann (1988). *Magical Means of Dealing with Ghosts in Ancient Mesopotamia*. PhD dissertation, University of Chicago.

Simpson, Jacqueline (2003). Repentant Soul or Walking Corpse? Debatable Apparitions in Medieval England. *Folklore* 114(3): 389–402.

Stratton-Kent, Jake (2016a). *Pandemonium: A Discordant Concordance of Diverse Spirit Catalogues*. Hadean Press.

Stratton-Kent, Jake (2016b) *A Prince Among Spirits*. Hadean Press.

Tanner, Marcus (2008). *The Raven King: Matthias Corvinus and the Fate of his Lost Library*. Yale University Press.

Tarrant, Neil (2020). Reconstructing Thomist Astrology: Robert Bellarmine and the Papal Bull *Coeli et terrae*. *Annals of Science* 77(1): 26–49.

Thorndike, Lynn (1923). *A History of Magic and Experimental Science*, volume II. Columbia University Press.

Timbers, Frances (2015). *The Magical Adventures of Mary Parish: The Occult World of Seventeenth-century London*. Truman State University Press.

Van der Laan, J. M. (2013). Faust from Cipher to Sign and Pious to Profane. In J. M. van der Laan and Andrew Weeks (eds.), *The Faustian Century*, 125–147. Camden House.

Wilby, Emma (2005). *Cunning Folk and Familiar Spirits: Shamanistic Visionary Traditions in Early Modern British Witchcraft and Magic*. Sussex Academic Press.

Index

www.ingramcontent.com/pod-product-compliance
Lightning Source LLC
Chambersburg PA
CBHW050841270326
41930CB00019B/3426